The personified
hook,

the entire
hypothetical
line
of BS
&

SYMBOLIC
SINKER!

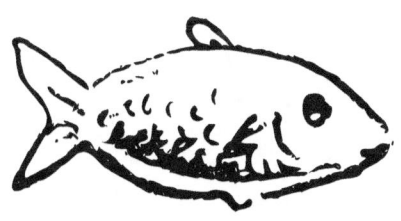

Author: Edmund W. Dalpe, MFA.

Editor Extraordinaire: Lori D. Dalrymple-Dalpe, M.Ed.

26,500 words, 174 pages, 36 illustrations.

Subject: Classic Fictional Satire: as an Epistemological Tragic Comedy.

Publisher: Dream Crow Ventures.

TABLE OF CONTENTS

THE NOOSE IS HANGING.

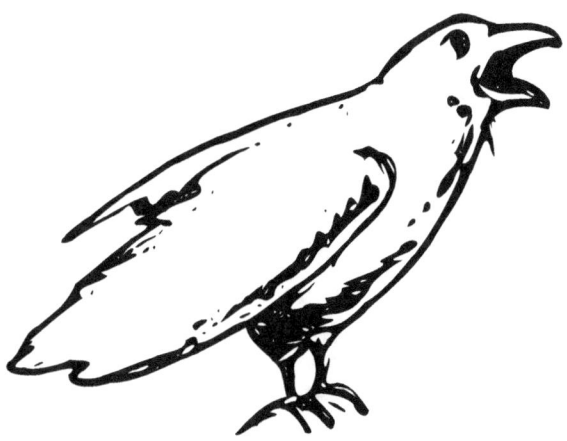

Beyond a shadow of a doubt, artists have always been on the team, but not a team that requires their mind be trained like a Tuffy Tool® in some academic's tool box. That's a bridge too too far for creative types.

Ironically, as the systems of those academically trained types have become fully autonomous, and as those systems now consider those crackerjack minded types as superfluous as they have considered artists over the millenniums, artists would be disingenuous if they told you they didn't find their social fraternity uproarious! After all, the misfortune of others does so warm our hearts; especially a karmic sequel.

Obviously, the law of unintended consequences appears to be thriving prodigiously. And the following event, is an exchange between two artists on that issue, whose ideas are pointedly germane, entertaining as all-get-out, and dare I say educational.

Without Further Ado:

All right, without further ado, let's begin the fastidious proceedings:

As witness and narrator of this audacious event, I would like to dedicate this momentous gathering to Mr. Samuel Langhorne Clemens, and everyone else that has at least one creative bone in their body.

Well … that's not the full verity of the matter. That idiot that once informed me that art is a lie, I fervently hope this soirée will cause you great consternation.

But, for everyone else … I, ahh … well … that's not entirely truthful either, academics are not excluded, after all, they're human beings.

However, unless they have a lot of hard bark on them, they may want to be quieter than a whore in church during the proceedings.

Yet, as far as I am concerned, academics are more than welcome to wax philosophical with this event's conversationalists, Becky and Tom, because I do enjoy the occasional cabaret.

Obviously, Becky and Tom are artists with fervid views. And the event I write about is an exchange between them, that I would describe as socially rudimentary to the times.

Expectedly, the objective of their deliberation, I would say is anything but academic.

Where the exchange took place is a non issue. It could have taken place in your home's living room, even the kitchen. The only essential elements needed were a few chairs, a lamp, a mini bar, and obviously a sandbox as an outlet for refreshments.

It wasn't a dialogue per se, it was more of a catch-as-catch-can series of complaints about 'all things', which they reduced to one single 'issue'. Which is the only thing typical about them.

You know, that singularity of focus that searches for that one pill to solve everything that ails them. Like most folks, they suffer from that same malady.

However, what's different, is what they focused on, which may very well be that one 'issue' to put the fix in on 'all things'.

Becky would say, "The 'issue' makes her feel like she's been rode real hard and put away wet!"

Becky, obviously is a Southern Bell, with no illusion about men's performance; present company excluded —naturally. She is about five foot nothing, medium build, medium height, medium everything. It's her passion that everyone finds most interesting about her. Which has always been the visual arts. Becky loves to paint and draw anywhere, anytime, about anyone and everything.

Becky's Grandma is always saying about her, "That girl is so creative, that I do declare, she could make a steaming pile come up smelling like a rose!"

Being intuitive, which Becky inherited from her Grandma, always gave her a home spun outlook about the nature of 'all things'.

Apparently, Becky became good friends with Tom because both had a creative attitude about everything.

Actually, it was Tom that initially took an immediate shine to Becky, because he saw in her his own reflection; albeit home spun, but himself nonetheless.

Tom is a portly man of average stature, is always well groomed, is amiable, but quick to ignite. He also is an artist, but his creations lean more toward literary works, because he is a bit more cerebral, which explains the short fuse.

Tom fine tuned his intuition to a science, which helps him to understand the most important thing about 'all things'.

Tom would often say, "That after millenniums, we really don't know a damn thing, we just figured out more ways to elaborate that point."

Which is the main reason Tom took a particular dislike with know-it-all academics. But, it is also the reason Becky finds Tom interesting. Being a Southerner, Becky is very fond of colorful thinking, and Tom's ambiguous answers appeals to Becky's sensibilities.

I would venture to say, the two of them combined understand human nature better then anyone I have ever met. And their nonchalant conversation opened my eyes to a new way of looking at their 'issue' about 'all things' that I will never forget.

For the adventurous type, their chat will introduce you to the rabbit hole! For the academic, pack your bags, because you're going on a guilt trip!

A Crack In Becky's Plaster.

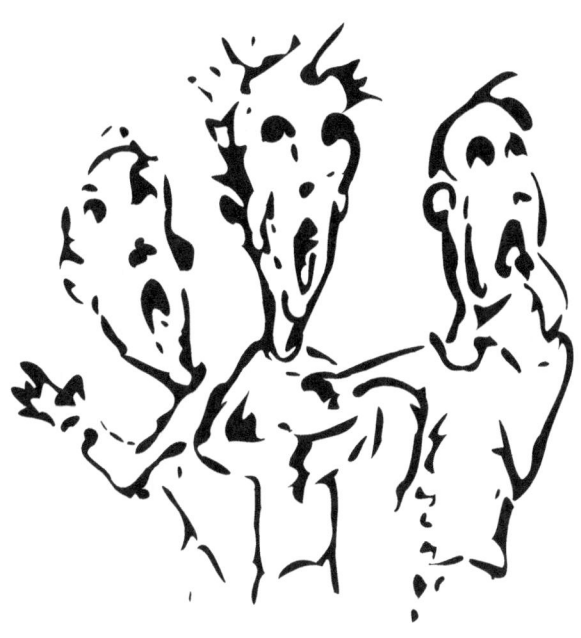

Because Becky trained her mind on how not to be trained, her thinking was unfamiliar to most folks. Consequently, Becky found her interest drifting from the Hoi Polloi's. She liked to chit chat about works of art, while others prefer nimble fingering their verbal salad on virtual pads.

Becky assumed it was nothing new. "Back in the day," she would say, "all they could speak about was the latest TV sensation that was integrated into their lives like a facsimile."

As far as Becky was concerned, the situation had nothing to do with the heat. She always said, "It's the humidity that makes them that way." Nor would Becky shy away from analogously illustrating the distinction when required. Becky would often say, "I find life is as pretty as a peach, while the others were avoiding it like a bastard at a family reunion."

However, being a considerate type, Becky did often modify her bold assertions. "Don't get me wrong," Becky would continue, "gregariously watching the grass grow on their virtual pads may have its merits, but I prefer the real thing over a simulacrum."

Becky always complained to Tom about the 'others,' as she called them. Most of the time they were brief outbursts and quickly resolved. However, her latest brouhaha was quite involved.

Tom, being a true friend, recognized Becky was in urgent need of a sounding board. Tom immediately sat down, slating whatever time was necessary for Becky's vexing issue.

The long harangue was not unlike a recent divorcee's riposte to a friend's polite question as to how their partner is doing!

Becky's Issue With the Others:

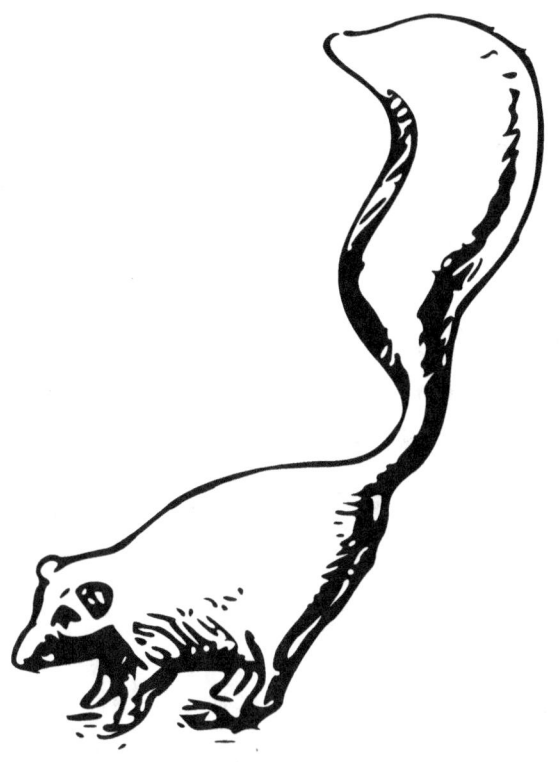

"Although it's not entirely clear as to why," Becky began, "I found that when I do make a human connection, and speak to the 'others' passionately about my interests, many get a funny look. It's a cockeyed gaze toward the ceiling with their eyes roaming about as if searching for cracks in my plaster. As such, I surmised it will be best for all concerned if I limit my intercourse to the amenities. I now greet them with a brief glance, a kind gentile smile and say, 'Wonderful day!'"

Hearing that, Tom chuckled, not simply because he came to the same conclusion, he also understood when a Southerner greets another in such a fashion, they were not being kind. Those are Southern expletives couched in politeness. Similar to the phrase, "Ain't you precious," both translate to … screwball, or something to that effect!

Nevertheless, Tom learned to carefully consider his audience when speaking. Especially, as creative thinking is alien to most folks. Visual artists, like Becky, tend to contemplate the beauty of a flower —while the 'others,' as Becky called them, are pondering the best way to eat it!

"However, there are times when I am preoccupied," Becky continued, "when I do often forget my interlocutor, and thus the situation can get … well, colorful. I would venture to say, the inevitable social discomfiture is a result of cultivating my mind on how not to be trained; while most of the 'others' mind's are trained what to think about incessantly. They're as busy as a cat on a hot tin roof, every minute of every day of their lives; K-12, College, TV, Movies, Cells, Net, News, War, Billboards, Radio, Plagues, Locust, and on and on ad infinitum!"

"Christ on a tricycle," Tom exclaimed, while shaking his head in disbelief!

"Consequently," Becky said, "because I know absolutely nothing about what preoccupies their mind, I get that cockeyed stare again. Apparently, I'm supposed to know whatever the latest distraction is that's rattling around in everyone's tin can. They call it the NEWS (North, East, West & South), I call it diddly-squat!"

"I hear you," Tom interjected. "However, they do occasionally show signs of life, with a sudden outburst of emotion from their usual rigor-mortise like gaze into their virtual pads. Whatever brought them momentarily back to the land of the living, I have about as much of an inkling as they do of my presence."

"You made my case," Becky returned. "They are oblivious to life. The distracted mind appears to atrophy, because of their mind training, and the more it is trained, the greater the entropy. It's as if their Religion is being obviated. I hate to be the bearer of bad news, but that's a hard dog to keep on the porch!"

As a point of interest, most of Becky's Southern analogous ways of expressively speaking are self explanatory ... well ... some are bewildering, and do stop us in our tracks, but, with a bit of imagination, we get the gist.

However, when Becky speaks about her Religion, she is referring to that thing she does with such passion. No. Not that one ... the one that most folks find mysterious about artists. Her friend Tom calls it his Mojo.

Being friends for sometime, Tom understood Becky's Southern way of speaking, which he enjoyed, and had a penchant to incorporate what he called 'Becky speak' into his own vocabulary. However, the manner in which he deployed it, Tom was the only one that thought it added color to his repertoire.

Interestingly, Becky's colorful expressions imbued in a rant are much more influential, and Becky being vexed, she was obviously being influential as all-get-out.

However, as Becky spoke as if her words were given some prior thought, because she did not appear to be frustrated, and as her ideas flowed without interruption, Tom interpreted that as Becky was looking to him for confirmation.

"I'm no ballerina," Becky continued, "yet, I am not entirely without skills. As a consequence of training my mind how to think, but not what to think about, I am good at problem solving, but lack the ability to implement solutions. In turn, I came to the realization that I have to find a way to open a dialogue with … well … the rest of the planet!"

Tom smiled, because he recognized the humor in Becky's dilemma and asked, "When did you first become aware of the communication 'issue'?"

"Well …," Becky answered, "I first recognized the démarche when I lost interest in thinking hypothetically about 'all things'. Because for most," Becky insisted, "such 'things' appear to occupy their thoughts almost entirely. De facto, I understood I lived in another world, which I did not find as a good or bad thing, as I view other ways of thinking stimulating, … well, intriguing ideas."

"And here is the interesting part," Becky pointed out with more intonation. "I also discovered, when I pressed the distracted mind for a response to my ideas, beyond their curious search for cracks in my ceiling, they were not amused!"

"Apparently," Becky confided, "my thinking is the antithesis of the big brains of the Hoi Polloi, called an academic, who passionately elucidate their disagreement with my line of inquiry, as the vein on their temple bulges during their risible diatribe. The chat is not unlike a reverend trying to bring a lost soul back to Jesus."

When Becky was particularly vexed, Tom, from experience, knew Becky would often expound on her analogous way of speaking with an additional comparison, to ensure her point was clearly made, which is the case at hand. Becky continued with … you guessed it, —a simile:

"I will simply suggest," Becky added, "the difference between the two minds can be pondered from the distinction between a Swiss watch, that's wound too tight, and a sundial."

Tom smiled at the additional comparison and reiterated what Becky stated thus far, "One is life, while the other is a simulacrum. Which supports what you stated earlier about their propensity to avoid life like a bastard being shunned at a family reunion."

"However," Tom suggested, "it appears to me, they could be oblivious to life, simply because of all of the distractions."

"That's possible," returned Becky. "However, it's not entirely clear. It may simply be they crave distractions, like a lush Jonesing for hooch, and to determine which, I need to find an answer to my dilemma. That being, how to open a dialogue with those academics and their distracted disciples, whose minds are apathetic, which is obviously problematic."

"After spending years racking my brain on how to do exactly that," Becky stated in a provocative manner, "one day, out of the blue, I had a eureka moment; crooning in the shower of all places. I felt washed clean, as if I was born again. Because the answer was as obvious as the brilliant sun streaming through the window that danced across the shower curtain."

"I realized, it was possible when the sun sets in the East," Becky stated with great determination!

Curiously, what Becky stated next was puzzling. It's not what Becky said that was unusual, it's how she said it. It was another characteristic of Becky being vexed. Similar to her double analogy, Becky would often perform what appeared to be a soliloquy in the middle of a conversation with others.

That unnerved most folks, as Becky would perform her literary device as if speaking over one shoulder, which made Becky's audience squint while frantically searching for whom she was speaking with.

Yet, Becky's soliloquies didn't bother Tom one iota, as experience had taught him, her attention would soon return. However, how long it took to return, Tom was able to gauge how vexed Becky was.

"After all," Becky said to herself, in a soliloquize like fashion, while gazing over her shoulder, "I didn't just fall off of the turnip truck!"

Tom, noticing Becky's literary device, understood she was still vexed. However, finding it humorous, he tried to conceal his amusement by taking a drink to hide his expression.

"The academic mind," Becky continued in her customary conversational manner, "that is the mind that trains the Hoi Polloi, may be inclusive of many cockamamie ideas, but how to think about them is definitely not one of them."

Hence, Becky conclusively declared in a resolute tone, "the dialogue will have to be more of a derisive monologue, for wasting years of my life racking my brain on an enigma!"

At that point, Tom could no longer conceal his amusement, he sprayed the contents he was nursing all over Becky, from his subsequent belly laugh. To which Becky was a bit bewildered, as she wiped her face of Tom's emotional cannonade, while exhibiting the same cockeyed look as the 'others.'

Tom responded to Becky's bewilderment by trying to control himself, and explain in an apologetic manner, "I'm not laughing at you."

Which everyone knows is not true, as the quagmires of others is the source of copious amusement. Nevertheless, Tom hypocritically assured her that the opposite was the case:

"I'm laughing" Tom stated, "because I'm still deeply immersed in that enigma, while you, in just a few short minutes resolved the 'issue.'"

Becky appeared to buy the crafted explanation, and began laughing herself. She was also tickled because she suddenly realized that she just unleashed a raster of shit on her friend. After which, Becky appeared to calm down and apologetically attempt to summarize the sum and substance of the matter.

"The point being," Becky surmised, "I find hypothetical conjecture healthy. What makes my butt itch is academia presenting their hypothetical ideas as facts, which is approximately 99.9% of what they claim, which their legions of disciples incessantly parrot as if gospel."

"Likewise," Becky stated, "it's their uppityness I take issue with. Like the know-it-all in every class, academia's modus operandi is to take ownership of 'all things', by defining everything, and thus framing the boundaries of permissible discourse, with very little understanding of the meaning of anything."

Tom, having patiently listened to all of Becky's concerns, and her determination, leaned back in his chair and pondered Becky's 'issue' for some time, but not before handing Becky a stiff drink, and another face towel —just in case.

Tom felt good about helping his friend, work it out as it were, and found it humorous how a sympathetic ear was all Becky really needed. And having similar interests and issues, Tom began to actively participate and bring up a few 'issues' of his own. Particularly, his vehement dislike for academics, which obviously the two shared.

They started to feed off of each other and what followed was a splendid banquet. The first course of which was academia's point of view of 'all things' served as an appetizer.

TOM'S HUMONGOUS MICRO

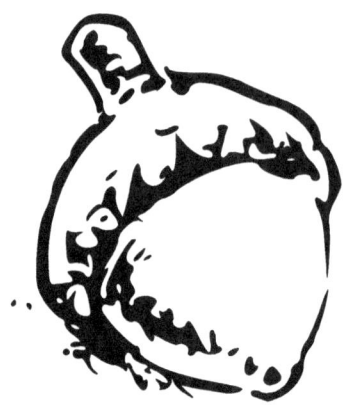

After contemplating Becky's concerns with great care, Tom was determined to shed greater light on the matter. That is, why the Jack of all trades, but master of none academic and their legions lack empathy.

Tom thought it would be a good idea to speak to Becky about academia's cosmology from his point of view. That is, from an artist's point of view; as an example of the profound differences between them. The idea was, from the comparison, something may glimmer through the ambiguous fog, which Tom confessed to Becky, "at the very least, it will be entertaining."

Becky, having unburdened herself was now receptive, even interested in what Tom had to say about the matter. She knew from past experience when Tom speaks about an issue, it is something he has given considerable thought.

"I could have picked any subject," Tom began, "it doesn't really matter, because they get annoyed with any of my ideas, academics that is. Specifically, I will briefly skim over an aspect of the Heliocentric model, where the planet Earth is a ball hurling through space, surrounded by an outer layer of gas, and immediately next to that is nothingness —a vacuum."

Tom emphasized, "I like to think of it as the immortal vacuum, because it's the same spooky monster that appeared on those Medieval maps depicting the abyss at the edge of the once known world."

"Apparently," Tom stated, in a conclusive voice, "the Heliocentric model simply reshaped Medieval cosmology from two to a three dimensional construct, transformed the language of 'all things' to be more systematically descriptive, while they iksnayed the speculative pizazz."

"What I found disturbing," Tom stipulated, "was not academia's uninspiring cosmology, it's their repackaging of the same old shtick, as being new and improved. Which means they really never abandoned flat Earth thinking, because they simply reshaped the boundaries of permissible discourse."

"Likewise," Tom continued, "with no self understanding about our true creative nature, that being our propensity to break the bonds of any boundary, which means they got the most important thing wrong, why should we listen to an academic about their point of view of anything?"

"Exploring our world should never be framed by anyone, especially with ideas that are excruciatingly boring," claimed Tom. "In the way a child views the color of the sky in awe, they need to be free to explore their world without telling them which way to look, and when they have questions, do not state your opinion as fact, as it undermines the creative process."

Tom's tone raised a bit when making the following point, "Learning is not about what, it's about how! Thus, memorizing the discoveries of others is meaningless. But, creating an environment that facilitates how those important discoveries were achieved, is what it's really all about."

"Consequently," Tom stated, "after only a few short years under academia's tutelage, a child's passion to explore their world is exsanguinated. It's like academics are spiritual vampires of the mind."

"I agree," Becky interjected. "And after several more years of scholarly training, if the fledgling eggheads had an original idea, it would die of loneliness."

"As such," Tom stated, "I think I have clearly established the ground from which my point of view of academia's uninspiring hokum propagates."

The Appetizer is Being Served.

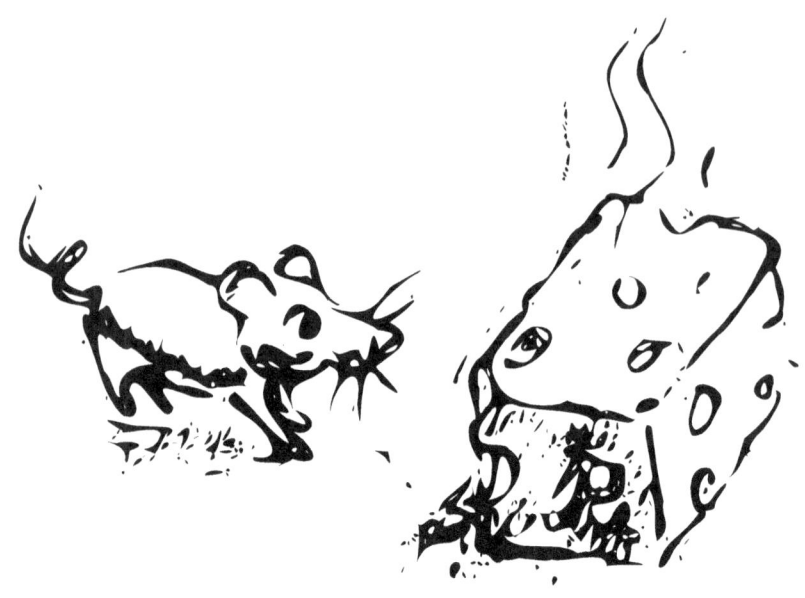

At that point Becky poured herself and Tom another drink and settled deep into her chair showing a genuine interest in what Tom was about to say, now that the preliminaries were out of the way. Becky understood Tom, being the cerebral type, could not go to the sandbox without contextualizing.

That frustrated most folks about Tom, but Becky having a laid back Southern way about her, could care less. In fact it amused her. When Becky was in search of entertainment, she would never ask Tom what he was doing, she would ask why he was doing it, from which Tom would contextually entertain Becky for some time. Becky would often extend the exposition, by sprinkling a few tactfully timed ifs, untils and howevers.

"All right, let's entertain a brief aspect of academia's cosmology," stated Tom, "because their ideas sap the life force out of my Mojo. Thus, we will keep our exposure to a minimum."

"As an example," Tom said, "during the 20th century, academia updated their wandering cosmology with a caveat of the big bang, which conveyed my mind back to a time, where I sat impatiently in an old mouldy class room, where a religious instructor informed us, it all began when God said, 'Let there be a brightly lit light.'"

"To-wit," Tom exclaimed, "BOOM, a hypothetical volcano exploded in Father Georges Lemaître pants, and thus 'all things' were violently ejected pell-mell, from which the universe expanded without end, while releasing much built up academic tension."

Becky interjected while smiling, "You're a blasphemous heathen!"

To which Tom returned, "It's the only way to illustrate their updated cosmology was in name only, because it's the same old flat Earth thinking of the Church, that was simply remolded, rebranded, repackaged and —relaunched with a big bang!"

"The issue with the big bada boom," Tom explained, "is it reestablished existence as being definitive, and thus having a beginning to 'all things', which brings theology front and center all over again, and runs contrary to my sense of the eternal. I don't buy it, nor did Einstein."

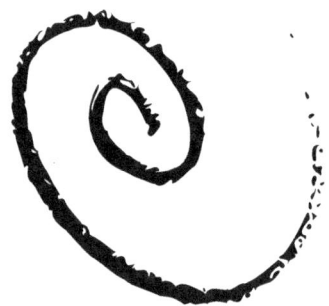

"Hypocritical … I mean … hypothetical conjecture that contradicts the nature of 'all things,'" stated Tom, "can't be taken too seriously, when all one has to do is look at nature's creative ingenuity, where the macro is revealed in the micro. Like the geometric shape and form of a nautilus shell, the formation of a galactic spiral would appear to reflect a similar Fibonacci like process; a slow, steady, harmonic growth, not the violent big bada boom dissonance of a dogmatic mind."

"So, there you have it," Tom stated. "That's my extremely brief riposte ... well, actually, let's call it the untrained, or unsullied mind's cosmological critical analysis of academia's point of view of 'all things', albeit not too complicated, and frankly, not terribly interesting. It's not a subject matter that gets my juices flowing. That is, hypothetically thinking about a hypothetical construct about a hypothetical idea."

"Jesus wept," retorted Becky.

Upon Tom's bewildered look, Becky immediately proclaimed, "No-no-no, don't get me wrong. I was fascinated with what you had to say. My exclamation was referring to your triple hypothetical somersault. That made my hair hurt."

Tom confided further, "There is a underlying reason their minds are so tightly wound."

"Obviously, we are not born that way," Becky responded. "Yet, for the life of me, I'm up-a-stump as to the underlying cause?"

Tom's voice became pallid when responding, "You are going to need another drink for what I'm about to tell you. In fact, you may want to make it a triple, because it will definitely uproot your tender follicles!"

Becky's Critique of Tom's Denunciation.

"Before you continue with the underlying cause, as to why the accredited mind is plumb cattywampus," Becky stated, "I would like to comment about what you have said thus far."

"The first thing I want to say," explained Becky, "is one of the reasons your critical analysis of academia's cosmology held my interest is, besides being brief, it's not like all of the 'others.' That is, you did not speak about what everyone else incessantly parrots. Thus, having the audacity to use your own noggin is admirable."

"Another difference between cosmologies," Becky continued, "and being your friend, obviously I am bias, there is a sense of meaning or grounding to your hypothetical thinking."

Tom felt the need to add, "I appreciate your point of view. Your objectivity is helpful. However, I understand that my ideas are a bit naive, because I never really gave it much thought beyond the ubiquitous compulsory mind training, to which we were all subjected."

"I'm not coddling you," returned Becky, "your idea of the micro revealing the macro makes a lot more sense to me than academia's jambalaya."

"Even when I was young," Tom said, "I could never get past their big bada boom. Ergo, everything that subsequently followed that original sprawling mélange, I considered it symbolic fruit, from the hypothetically poisonous tree."

"I agree," returned Becky. "You can't build a foundation in a swamp."

"Nevertheless," Becky explained, "the third difference in your way of thinking, was how you expressed your point of view, as not being definitive, and you presented it in such a way that stimulates further inquiry. After all, the subject matter is hypothetical, and will remain an open question."

"I agree," Tom said, "but there is also a fourth difference, which has to do with the inspirational issue you mentioned."

"As an artist," stated Tom, "my voice and ideas are created from lived experience, the knowledge inherent in being, emotional intuition, imagination, and all of my senses."

"However," continued Tom, "the academic mind is bound to its system, where each subsequent hypothesis exists within its functional framework. Because that is precisely with whom I was speaking, and whose ideas I was challenging —the system's!"

"That's very astute," stated Becky, "making that subtle distinction in voice. Considering, that we are trained to explore exclusively within the system's permissible boundaries, which is a quasi voice at best, we confuse the system's logic for our own voice!"

"I would say so," Tom responded, "which explains why academics perceive my challenge as a personal affront. 'Oh Pardon' me,' I would say, 'was that your hunch I just stepped in?'"

"Consequently," Tom stated, "a bewildered countenance overtakes their pejorative academic glare, not unlike a doe frozen in the headlights, which is my cue to get while the gettin's good."

Becky began laughing so hard she found her eyes needing the face towel Tom gave her during the last emotional episode. She hysterically fell backwards into her chair, spilling her drink in the process.

PICKING HYPOTHETICAL DAFFODILS.

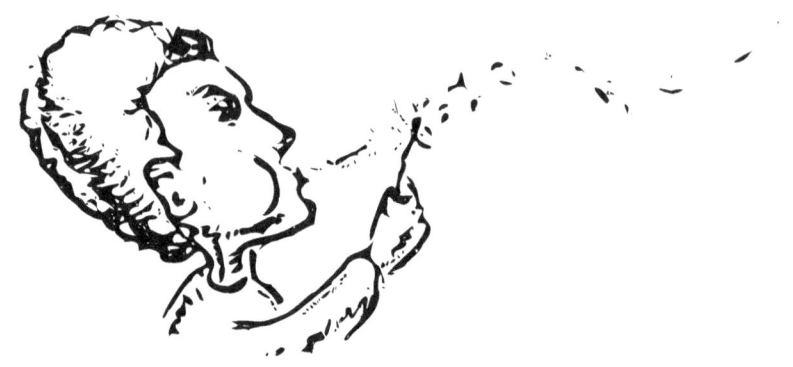

"Now that you have regained your composure," Tom said, "I will now present you with a plausible explanation as to why the academic mind is wound way too tight, and in the process uproot your tender follicles."

"All right," returned Becky, "proceed," she said while running her fingers through her coiffure, making sure nothing fell out!

"The primary distinction between the metaphorical and hypothetical minds," stated Tom, "is the former never goes out on a hypothetical limb without metaphorical cause."

"What is the metaphorical," asked Becky coyly?

"You would ask me that," stated Tom, "I'll see if I can find the words."

"OK," Tom said. "Let's call a metaphor a phenomenological way of seeing. It's not the thing per se, let's call it the root mind's way of beholding its world."

"Interesting," Becky said. "Call it an abstract state of mind, because we all share the same experiential understanding about the nature of things. Like how cirrus clouds infer ambiguousness, while a single rock all by it lonesome infers thingness."

"Oppositely," Tom said, "that is not how the trained mind functions. The operative word is — trained. They are repeatedly conditioned how to look and think about 'all things' in context to a hypothetical mind system of rules, processes and procedures, void of a metaphorical pulse."

"Academia is the Peter-Principle of ideas," stated Tom, "where each successive hypothetical patch in a line of thinking gets more and more outlandish, like the big bada boom! They believe their definition of 'all things' holds meaning; between the lines as it were, from an amalgamation of its hypothetical aggregate. But the verity of the matter is, the system is conversing with itself, in an ever evolving form of sameness!"

"They're bound in a nutshell," Becky said, "yet arrogantly consider themselves intellects of infinite space, which gives me bad dreams …"

"Yea," returned Tom, "the dream from which none awakes, —in an eternal systematic slumber! The sovereign mind is not a flute to be played in a hypothetical ballad. It speaks exclusively in metaphorical terms."

Becky seemed very intrigued and asked Tom to expound on how the creative mind thinks and builds metaphorical meaning; "Not in the obvious manner," Becky stipulated, "every child knows what is and is not interesting, but how our mind builds a conceptual understanding of its world."

The Hind, Lioness, Snake & Boar.

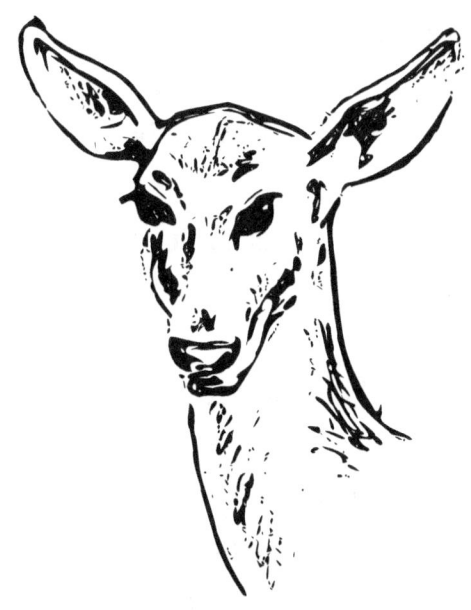

"Well," Tom said, "we all know life is a learning experience, from which we are able to recognize and express our awareness of the eternal, like imagining a hind in the pattern of a tree's bark, or in our dreams; no schooling is required to socially express that concept via metaphorical imagery."

"Deer are depicted on most coat-of-arms to socially communicate that awareness," Tom said. "Even though, back in the day, the Hoi Polloi confused the male for the female. It's the hind that conveys the generational aspect of the eternal, not the stag."

"From the Pre-Socratics forward," Tom pointed out, "metaphorical thinking in the Occident has become incrementally abased. The Greeks were notorious in that endeavor, like their personification of the eternal hind with Artemus."

"Apparently," stated Becky, "the Greeks had a cultural agenda."

"They sure did," Tom stated.

"Regardless," Tom said, "our creative mind, that is its imaginative aspect, speaks analogously about what it perceives in relationships."

"We build our understanding from life," Tom said, "not a system, threading what is metaphorically inferred from our experiences into meta-theories, which then we are able to apprehend the larger context from the Cartesian aggregate, like our non-Cartesian awareness of the eternal, expressed as a hind."

"Hold your horses," Becky said. "When you mention Cartesian and non-Cartesian thinking, I am not following your meaning in context to art. Define the distinction between them, if you would."

"Sure," Tom said. "The Cartesian mind is goal oriented, like balancing your bank account. It uses behavioral mind conditioning like muscle memory in sports. We memorize —9x9=81. We don't think about it, we belch it out as if instinctual. It's a mind-set that has no probative value, because it's limited to practical thinking."

"It is our evolutionary strategy," stated Tom. "Humans are not born with an ability like flight, we are born with a creative capacity to develop any ability. Thus, each generation must learn to develop their own unique strategy, which our Non-Cartesian mind, that is creative thinking, is designed to metaphorically assist the Cartesian mind in that endeavor, because it has probative value."

"However," Tom stipulated, "as the social strategy is to train everyone to be a useful tool, we dwell in a hypothetical mental box, and as the trained tool speaks a hypothetical language, which is essentially nonsense to the natural mind, the social strategy undermines our amazingly creative evolutionary design."

"Call me silly," stated Becky, "but I would think augmenting, not undermining, our creative evolutionary strategy would make more sense."

"It sure would," Tom said, "but, apparently, that is not expedient."

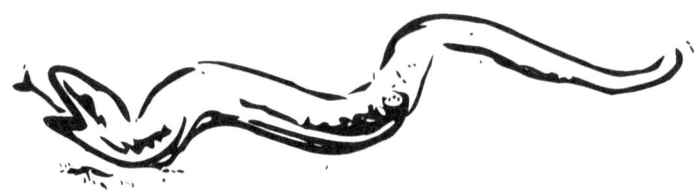

"The metaphorical mind expresses such consequential actions as a snake," stated Tom. "That is to say, training the Cartesian aspect of one's mind with a hypothetical mind system molds it into a Tuffy Tool®, which undermines its creative capacity —then after thousand of years the system has produced a culture teaming with hybrids, who are about as useful as they are creative, because AI can perform a Tuffy Tools'® function, —and as the pace of tech is shorter than the required training period, academia is also obsolete, as only AI can keep pace with tech — respectively, academia will now become a religion, and preach AI social dogma, and so on and so forth in a meandering run-on, all of which is to say snake."

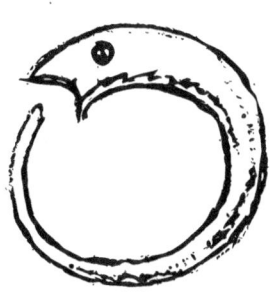

"Wow," responded Becky with a look of astonishment! "That's a self devouring snake."

"Nevertheless," continued Becky, "it makes sense; snake that is, not their social insanity. However, just to be sure I understand how to express that idea in a hybrid's language, define how a snake metaphorically conveys that consequential manner of thinking."

"Contrary to academic thinking, all beings do not have knowledge, they are knowledge," said Tom. "Metaphorically speaking, each being is an abstract expression of, … well … let's call them domains of knowledge, like a bird is knowledge of the sky, because its entire evolutionary trajectory evolved in context to that environment. Hence, bird metaphorically infers knowledge of the overview, because it's a sky being."

"Likewise," Tom continued, "as the snake moves in a serpentine rhythmic manner, the snake's knowledge metaphorically speaks of cognitive interconnectivity, which then infers augmented knowledge, i.e., this idea finds sway from its antecedents."

"Can a snake be used as a metaphorical expression for language," Becky asked?

"No," Tom answered, "snake does not express languaging. In metaphorical terms, we first need to express languaging before expressing its product."

"Right," stated Becky. "You previously made that distinction between the two minds; that the creative mind does not hypothetically hypothesize."

"Exactly," stated Tom, "Unlike the systematically trained mind, the metaphorical mind does not speak of memorized hypothetical things, because the natural mind can not speak of something that it has not first metaphorically established, which means it has to actually perceive it and likewise be able to visually expresses it. Thus, artists do not speak or think in 'hypothetical words,' we are in the business of forming new 'words' on the root level, as Merleau-Ponty understood."

"So," Becky said, "to answer my own question, there is no meaning in a metaphor except for what it directly infers in any given context."

"Yes," said Tom, "However, it's understandable how you made that leap, because I do the same thing. To suggest the snake infers languaging, is to use a metaphor as a symbol; as a knee jerk reaction from our systematic mind training."

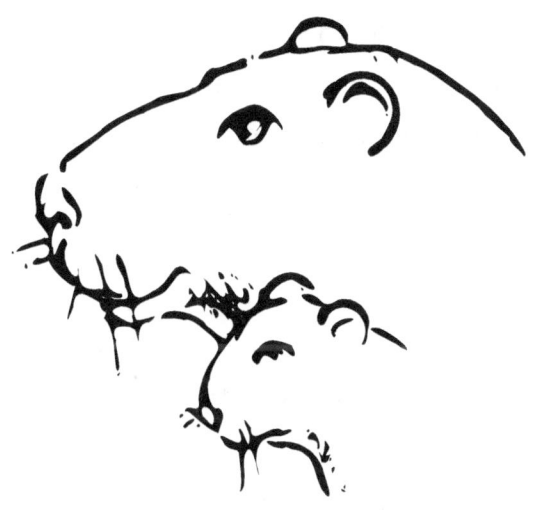

"Metaphorically," Tom said, "a lion is used to express languaging, not a snake, because among beings cats are peerless when it comes to memory. Cats are the beings that do not forget. Hence, the lion metaphorically conveys knowledge of a tenacious memory. That is the metaphorical meaning of <u>Lion-Man</u> of Hohlenstein-Stadel Cave in Germany, dated 38,000 B.C. —Language!"

"However," Tom said, "like their Greek progenitors, academia has an agenda. They deliberately got the sex wrong to keep the Hoi Polloi metaphorically ignorant, because, … well, … let's just say the metaphorical mind is not as malleable as one that is hypothetically trained to be a tool. After all, to a hammer, everything looks like a nail."

"It is the lioness that expresses language," Tom stipulated, "because she is a metaphorical expression of the idea about generational knowledge of tenacious memory, which expresses language in the sense you mean, not the male lion."

"Likewise, Tom said, "as the systematically trained mind is indifferent to their metaphorical faculties, because the hypothetical and metaphorical are mutually exclusive mind-sets, thus the trained tool is oblivious to the Lion-Man having a vulva, and ignorant of the metaphorical fact that only a lioness can be an expression of language."

"Right," interjected Becky, "as you pointed out, academia's hybrids are trained to think in the same e-pluribus-unum hive-minded principality, void of creative independent thought."

"To paraphrase Yogi Berra," Becky said, "if you talked to one hybrid, don't bother looking for a second opinion, because 'it will just be déjà vu all over again!'"

"Hold on a second," Becky stated in surprise "I just had what you might call a vu-jà-dé moment!"

"What's the hell is vu-jà-dé," asked Tom?

"It's the opposite of dé-jà-vu," Becky said. "It means, I actually learned something new, because I had a strange feeling of experiencing something I have never encountered before —ever; that being, what you just inferred with the date of 40,000 years ago!"

"Are you saying that language was Neanderthal's mind-tech," asked Becky?"

"Absolutely," Tom said. "It's indisputable. Languaging, not to be confused with the ability of most animals to communicate in the immediate context, that is to say, metaphorically abstract visual thinking, was established more than forty millenniums ago on the European continent, six millenniums prior to when Cro-Academia wandered aimlessly into the region."

"Well butter my butt and call me a biscuit," exclaimed Becky! "That would explain a lot of things. Creative types could be a different species!"

"Do you think that's the reason why the 'others' are … you know … the way they are," asked Becky?

"To be honest," Tom said, "it's not entirely clear if it's genetic, or caused by their synthetic mind training, or if it is a consequence of their cultural environment that mercilessly distracts them from developing their natural mind. Then again, it could be all of the above."

"To reveal how metaphorically ignorant the hypothetically trained mind is," Tom stated. "Cro-Academia sent legions of their brightest and best descending into the Paleolithic caves of Europe with their magnifying glasses to analyze the calcium build up on the paint to determine the age of the so called art, when all they had to do is read the dates written on the walls."

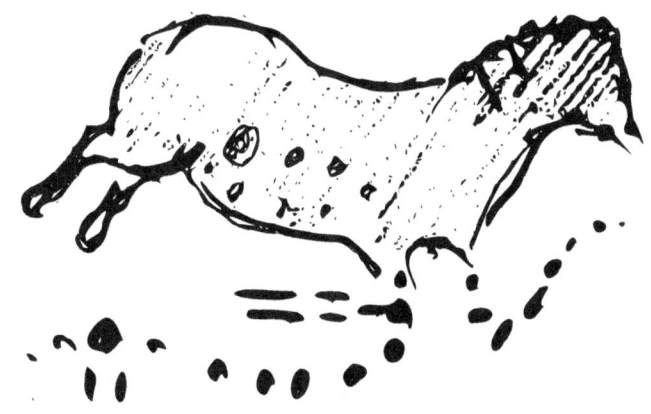

"This illustration from Lascaux," Tom stipulated, "spoke of a date range of about 2.5 millenniums that began when Alderamin was the polestar to when Deneb would take its place."

"That's hilarious," stated Becky, as she got up to stretch her legs and refresh their drinks. While filling Tom's glass, she stated, "It's also perplexing that the 'others' dream the same metaphorical lingo, but don't understand a damn thing!"

"As I said, the Hoi Polloi's mind is trained not to understand metaphorical abstractions, because the two minds are like water and oil; they do not mix," Tom said. "Ergo, as their trained mind is locked in silly mode, they can't understand what language is, because language can only be understood on the root level. Likewise, when they try to explain language, i.e., 'lioness', they start rolling around hilariously chasing their own tail."

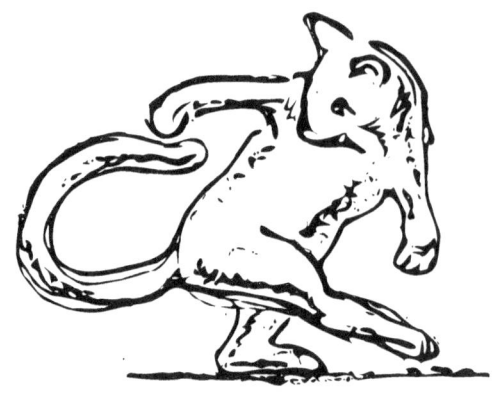

"That's a perfect metaphorical expression for the hypothetically trained mind," Becky interjected. "That is a cat, which is to say language, chasing its systematic tail."

"Nevertheless," Tom said, "to express your idea of mind-tech, we would need to infer the lioness passing her reflections from one generation to the next as a technological process, like drawings in a library for every generation to read. A cave would be a perfect venue, which necessarily requires those reflections to be couched in expressions of relative time."

"The Paleolithic cave of Chauvet in France," Tom said, "communicates that exact social process with absolute metaphorical clarity, which is explained in great detail in Edmund Dalpe's magnum opus titled, <u>Dream Duet</u>."

"For the natural mind," said Tom, "or artist, if you will, a being is knowledge. Yet, for the hypothetically trained mind or hybrid, knowledge is found in the arrangement of symbols in a mind system, which is a hypothetical construct that's not real, which makes their trained mind trip the light fantastic."

"What an artist thinks of as a metaphorical expression," Tom stipulated, "the hybrid calls a symbol. What an artist denotes as imagination, the hybrid defines as reasoning, and what the artist recognizes as causality, the hybrid calls the system's logic. One is technological and the other is biological."

"Apparently," Becky said, "the hybrid is so mentally confused that even a good shag becomes a non-binary simulacrum!"

"I am curious," Tom asked, "I don't think I ever had … ahh … you know … one of those!"

"One of what," asked Becky?

"A non-binary," exclaimed Tom, while blushing! "How about you show me how that works?"

"Sure," responded Becky, "go outside and get me a switch, and I'll give ya some sugar!"

"Well," Tom said, as his face became pale, "I ahh … on second thought, I think we should stick with the theoretical … for now."

"All right," said Becky, as both began to laugh.

"Just as hilarious, is when an academic explains creativity," Tom said, "because the trained mind's system of languaging is a technological mind system that supplants imagination with the system's logic."

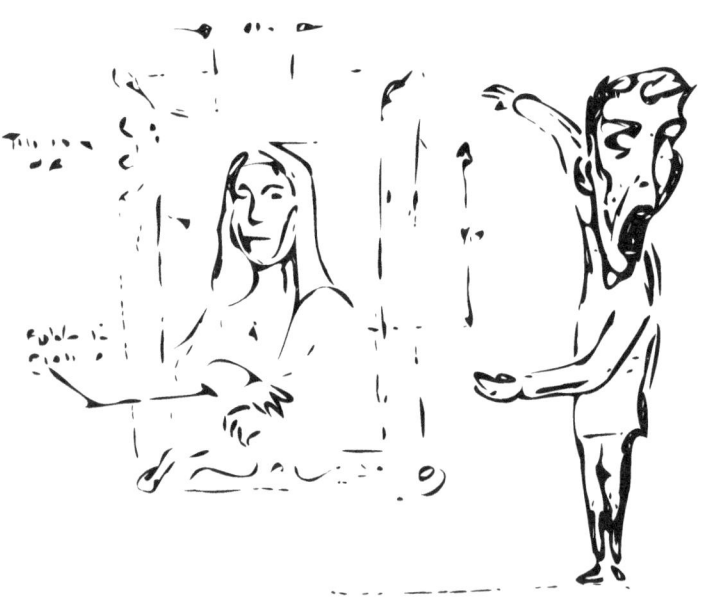

"Hence," Tom said, "when an academic speaks of art, which is really languaging, they get strange. I mean downright monotone spooky."

"Well," returned Becky, "that explains why the Greeks and their academic offspring mangle the meaning of seminal metaphors beyond recognition. The Hoi Polloi's pea picking minds are being metaphorically shucked."

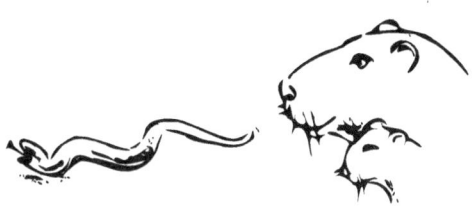

"All right," Becky said. "Let me try that again. If I associate an image of a lioness with a snake, I'm speaking of historical knowledge, which no longer speaks of lioness or snake. The association creates a new inference."

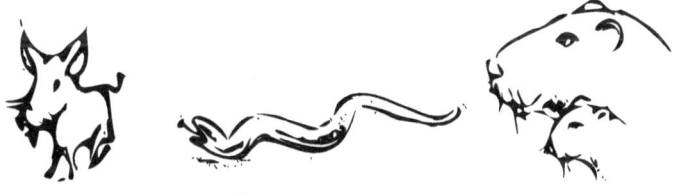

"Yes," Tom responded, "and if we add another metaphor, it will give us the context of what particular genre. For example, if I add the boar, which is knowledge of the Earth, I am metaphorically speaking of historical knowledge of the Earth."

"And 40 thousand years into the future," Becky pointed out, "every human whose mind wasn't academically bushwhacked will understand your meaning."

"True," stated Tom, "which explains why a hybrid goes cockeyed with metaphorical thinking. A mind trained to believe that the sounds of their language holds meaning, and they accept that without question, translates to a religious belief system."

"Predictably," Tom stipulated, "when I ask the trained mind to express sounds that convey the abstract concept of, 'Historical knowledge of the Earth,' hilariously, the really dumb and smart ones will literally say, 'Historical knowledge of the Earth.' But, when most suddenly recognize that sounds can not express abstract ideas, they get angry, because that's what happens when one challenges religious myths."

"We have to be careful," Becky said, "by showing a hybrid how to use their natural mind, they could develop their own way of languaging and voice independent of the hive-mind, which could dissolve the cohesion of the social system."

"I doubt it," Tom said. "Everything would work out just fine. The arts would socially assume their rightful intellectual status. Obviously, oligarchs would be out of work, and academia will be limited to a trade school's curriculum of 'technique' —but who cares, so long as they remain in their hypothetical ditch where they belong! And when they come up with their next scheme, it will fall on deaf ears, because in education the arts will be managed by artists not academics."

"However," Tom stipulated, "our metaphorical intellect is not a secret. Hybrids have had access for millenniums. They can make the connection between the two minds any time they want. But, I don't believe they would venture out on their own, which is the reason I suspect we are dealing with another species. They are uncomfortable around people that think different from them, even belligerent, which means they feel threatened. That's not a result of mind training, that's instinctual behavior —that is, schooling, flocking and herding!"

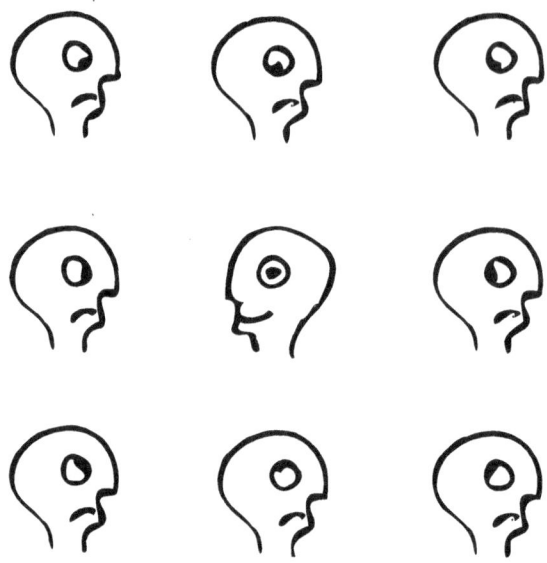

"That makes sense," stated Becky, "and it explains their intolerance to creative ideas and why they all parrot the same damn thing. Their evolutionary stratagem appears to be quantitative not qualitative."

"Returning to our natural mind," Tom said, "a metaphor holds an array of ideas. Thus, a bird is not limited to expressing knowledge of the overview. Like when birds scatter on a tree-line, that tell us something is a foot in the forest. Hence, bird also infers knowledge of what is imminent. However, when a metaphor is associated with another metaphor the array of various meanings of both metaphors becomes limited by the association."

"Thus," Tom stipulated, "abstract metaphorical language and thinking is all about context. A snake's inferred meaning refers to this here, and it means that there, thus a snake's inferred associative meaning is different everywhere."

"That's the reason we do not perceive our world literally," continued Tom. "We also see imaginatively, because our imagination speaks of a larger context when we perceive. We apperceive, because we are the being that imagines."

"Well, I do declare," exclaimed Becky loudly! From Tom's statement, Becky appeared to have another vu-jà-dé moment. She realized why she was so annoyed when she read Plato's Republic a while back.

"Apparently," stated Becky, "that's what got Plato's toga in a twist —imagination. However, he lied like a rug in that regard, as well as issuing outrageous death threats to artists whose thinking did not comply with his opinion."

"We find the same mentality in ancient Mesopotamian art," said Becky, "that is replete with the motif of the killing of lions, which metaphorically reveals an intolerance for a way of thinking, and as Mesopotamia is the origin of Cro-Magnon, that supports the theory that the hive-mind is instinctual."

"Academics have the same obnoxiously intolerant mentality about metaphorical imagination," returned Tom, "because the natural mind can only be hypothetically shackled, if it is bamboozled, or in Plato's case, threatened."

"I wouldn't be surprised if Plato's <u>Allegory of the Cave</u> was a cunning scheme hiding in plain sight to bury the human mind in a hypothetical maelstrom," stated Becky.

"Agreed," Tom stated, "I have no doubts about it, because the hypothetical mind is not able to see and think with its born faculties. If it could, academia's bogus definition of <u>Lion-Man</u> would never pass the sniff test, because whomever made such a proposal would not be taken seriously."

"More importantly," Becky asked, "why is academia meddling in the metaphorical domain to begin with?"

"Well," responded Tom, "that's what they do. They never stay in their hypothetical ditch where they belong. From the pre-Socratics forward they deliberately muck-up the metaphorical in order to obviated non-Cartesian thinking. They want a Cartesian tool that can barely think."

"For the natural mind," Tom said, "non-Cartesian thinking, that is imagination, supports or invalidates its Cartesian way of being mindful, and vice versa; they are different sides of the same cognitive coin."

"That's how the mind naturally resolves issues," Tom continued, "which is most apparent in the manner we dream, because our biological mind does what it was designed to do —be imaginatively probative. It can not be trained to do otherwise."

"However," Becky stated, "as the Hoi Polloi's Cartesian aspect of their mind is mercilessly distracted, the hypothetical mind appears to be a by-product of classical Pavlovian behavioral conditioning, trained to react to stimuli; ring the bell for class and they all start systematically salivating."

The Delta and its Wine Dark Sea.

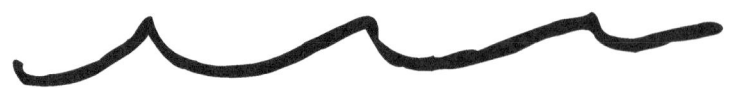

"The most fundamental example of the mind conditioning of the Hoi Polloi," stated Tom, "is the Greek oligarch and military commander Thales' personification of the water metaphor."

"How is Thales' personification of the water metaphor, from thousands of years ago, relevant with today's conditioning of the human mind," asked Becky?

"Hypothetically speaking," Tom said, "for the artificially trained mind, knowledge is a systematic process. They were socially trained how to perform addition long before they are trained to multiply, because the latter is built from the former. Which means today's systematic mind training occurs in historical stages, paralleling their social development over millenniums, beginning with the stone age —kindergarten!"

"Thus," Tom stipulated, "Thales' first-grade curriculum is as relevant today as it was millenniums ago."

"Thales' personification of the water metaphor was/is an assault on the kernel of the creative mind," continued Tom, "because water is the metaphorical expression of our mind thinking about its vast reservoir of non-Cartesian memories, ebbing and flowing from, dare I say, the logos of embryonic ontogenesis, to each lived experience in the wine dark sea, if you will."

"Likewise," Tom said, "the natural human mind situates its memories, in a vast metaphorical Delta, where the mind's fluid expressions are intertwined in an earthly aroma, teaming with metaphorical life, where even things like meadows and forests speak to us in an analogously anecdotal fashion."

"When we imagine water," continued Tom, "our mind is doing what it is designed to do —being imaginatively probative. Thus, contemplations in the Delta are philosophical reflections of a mind engaged in worldness."

"However," Tom stated, "being a Greek trickster Thales personified the Delta's water metaphor, by projecting said metaphorical expression for thinking about 'all things' to the nature of 'all things,' no different than Artemus personifying the eternal. Both are crafted to humanize 'all things' and thus muck-up the metaphorical mind in order to claim ownership and control of the Delta."

"If I am recalling correctly," Becky interjected, "academia situates Thales as one of the first academic thinkers in all of human history, because he reckoned the nature of 'all things' as holding the characteristic of water in an embryonic academic system of mind."

"Thales was a military commander," stated Tom, "not the sainted deep thinker academia advertises. The water shtick by oligarchs predates Thales. Most oligarchs of that time claimed they could walk on water, while others claimed to be its source."

"Metaphorically,"Becky said, "they were claiming to be rulers of the Hoi Polloi."

"Precisely," stated Tom. "It was a time when all humans spoke metaphorically. Hell, read the Bible, it's nothing but metaphorical expressions, where some dude gets swallowed by a great fish, which metaphorically means he had a life altering change in his Delta's thinking."

"Fish is the water being," Tom said, "that is constantly changing as it darts. As such, the fish speaks of knowledge of change in the Delta, that is to say, an evolution of mind. Hence, the fish or water being metaphorically infers learning."

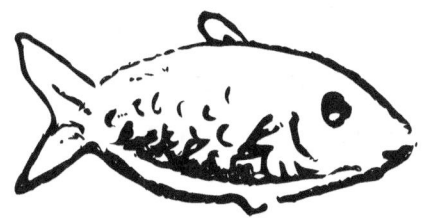

"However," interjected Becky, "to imagine such a big fish, they must have had a mind altering upheaval!"

"Exactly," said Tom, "It doesn't make sense. The creative process is not a sudden gargantuan enlightenment, like being baptized in a magical Delta and reborn into a know-it-all mind."

"That's not how the creative process works," Tom stated. "Learning requires actual hard work, because it is about making small Cartesian connections in building a larger non-Cartesian awareness, like our awareness of the eternal hind."

"That tells us the dude that got swallowed by a big fish," said Becky, "was an oligarch's manufactured fable. Like a pope that likes to parade around in their big fish hats, which is to metaphorically claim their mind is the source of Delta knowledge, no different than Thales."

"Absolutely," responded Tom. "It's academia's foundational pond rippling myth. Like I said, hypothetical thinking is only possible if the metaphorical mind gets bamboozled!"

"I have had countless dreams of water beings," Tom said, "I encountered in the depths of the wine dark sea as brilliant as an aquamarine gemstone. I even rode on the backs of humongous fish. But, I was never consumed by a water being, nor did I ever fear them, because that runs contrary to their metaphorically edifying nature."

As Becky was giving her closing remarks about the big-fish sermon, Tom was quite animated, shaking his head in the affirmative, while rolling his eyes upward as if to say to Becky, no surprises there.

"Without a doubt," Becky surmised, "the big-fish story it's more water-walking hokum. Because it's stating that the mind's learning process was so overwhelmed by what it had discovered that it devoured its own mind!"

"Obviously," Tom said, "it's an oligarch's nonsensical myth, crafted to engender fear of learning, so that the Hoi Polloi would entrust such dangerous matters to a Zen water walking master! They are all about dumbing the human mind down. And after several millenniums of their tutelage, as you well know Becky, it's a shocking experience conversing with a schooled Hoi Polloi whose mind has been Humpty Dumped."

"I can imagine the public spectacle in the forum of a local hamlet," stated Becky, "where Thales trotted out some buffoon from another region dribbling in his porridge as proof. You know, leave the thinking to the professionals with the big brains, or this could happen to you too."

"Water metaphorically translates to imagination," Tom said, "which is creative thinking. Thus, Thales' personification of the water metaphor to 'all things' was claiming to be the ideas man, that he was the source of all knowledge and thinking, no different than every other water walking, dowser perambulating, fish hat wearing oligarch before him and every subsequent academic since."

"Thales was not the first," stated Tom, "nor will he be the last Zen water master to stir up mud by mucking about in the metaphorical Delta."

"Academia's latest Delta assault," stated Tom, "is an attempt to blur the metaphorical distinction between the sexes. Like water, the dualistic sex metaphor is at the core of our metaphorical language and mind, because it's a human being's fundamental syntax."

"Two questions," Becky interjected. "The first is, what's the connection between Thales' personification of the water metaphor and academia's sexual assault on language? And the second is, how is sex metaphorically syntactical?"

"Obviously," Tom said, "both sex and syntax are about making connections. But, let's shelve that idea for the moment, considering you like to play with switches!"

"OK," said Becky, "as her eyes lit-up, while trying not to smile."

"To address the former first," Tom said, "as we are conceived and have evolved within the water of our mother's womb, when the human mind speaks of water, it's imagining memories of being, that is, thinking about its Delta; they are one and the same, in the same way, a female deer metaphorically expresses the eternal in a generational non-Cartesian manner about being in time; again the Delta."

"In so far as the syntactical significance of the distinction between male and female knowledge of any being," stated Tom, "the former speaks of Cartesian knowledge and the latter speaks of generational knowledge in time in a non-Cartesian way, which necessarily is a central distinction to make for the being that imagines, when speaking to another or to themselves. That is to say, are we speaking of experiential knowledge recalled, or an imagined idea about what may be over the horizon?"

"For example," said Tom, "a drawing of a colorful male snake speaks of the idea that came from a connective cognitive process. However, the less colorful female snake, who is by far more interesting, she speaks about the connective process in that context, not its product. The former is Cartesian and the latter non-Cartesian thinking."

With a look of pensiveness, Becky stated, "I am starting to realize that academia's assaults on the creative mind have the real potential to destroy a culture, because they are assaulting the metaphorical root."

"Absolutely," stated Tom. "The trained mind is not consciously aware of the meaning of metaphorical expressions. Yet, on an unconscious level they are affected by virtue of being human — sort of. For the trained mind it's like an unlocked back door to their mind."

"Thus," Tom said, "academia's metaphorical assaults makes the Hoi Polloi go crazy, but they don't know why; like a prankster putting itching powder in somebody's paints. It's the trained mind's Achilles' heel, which is why Plato attacked the arts, and the same reason academia will never stop attacking our Delta."

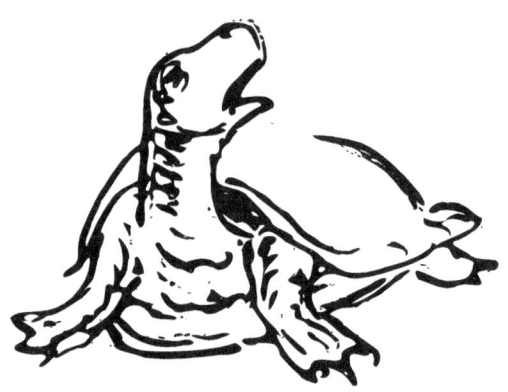

"Likewise," stated Becky "oligarchs and their academics periodically incite metaphorical chaos, which is not possible with a culture teaming with creative types, because our mind has natural armor. They can't manipulate a developed metaphorical mind, which is why they benevolently fund schools for toddlers."

"Academia's intrigues are by the numbers," continued Tom. "First deflower the distinction between the sexes by replacing the hind with the stag, then devour vis-a-vis its personification to the androgenous Artemus; whose shifting human moods and character are carefully crafted social narratives to manipulate the Hoi Polloi."

"They combined the two assaults and the kitchen sink," Tom said, "with the personification of the Mind-Eternal (language) into a Being-Eternal (God), who begat an androgenous man-god that shed his menstrual water and died in an unnatural childbirth while delivering an adorable newborn bouncing eternal realm. Which subsequently resurrected the yo-yo in a Sisyphus like unending life and death cycle of the seasons."

"Each of academia's machinations," Becky said, "are crafted to obliterate the human mind's metaphorical connection with their Delta."

"As such," Tom stated, "Thales' personification of the mind's metaphorical expression for thinking, was crafted to divide the human mind from its innate cognitive process, to conquer and subdue its creative will."

"That's what an academic education is," Becky stated, "to 'civilize' the creative mind, because there is nothing more problematic than a human being that knows how to think on the root level in the language of the ages, and thus independent of the hive-mind system."

"That's the reason the hypothetical mind is missing an ore in their boat ride," suggested Becky.

"Absolutely," Tom responded, "no question about it. By muddying the mind's water metaphor, and blurring its sexual syntax, with their infinite manifestations and intrinsic relationship between mind and world, the human mind becomes estranged from its innate cognitive reflections. Likewise, it becomes rudderless, and thus pliable."

"Academic thinking doesn't happen naturally," stated Tom. "You have to actually muddy up the metaphorical mind beyond recognition to confuse the mind's metaphorical expression about its philosophical reflections, as the nature of 'all things.'"

"That's plumb stupid," stated Becky with a look of surprise!"

"I never accused Thales of being stupid," responded Tom. "Like Plato, he was as cunning and manipulative. We have to remember who we are dealing with. They are gift bearing Greeks!"

"Why would anyone listen to such rubbish," Becky asked with a look of astonishment?

"Well," Tom said, to paraphrase W. C. Fields, who was paraphrasing Lincoln, 'You can fool some of the people all the time —and that's enough to make a decent living.'"

"It's the same way academia inverts the creative process," Tom stated, "by teaching children what to hypothetically learn, but never showing them how to metaphorically discover; especially their Delta. Thales and his academic progeny favor a dependent and pliable human mind refashioned to perform mundane tasks —you know, a Tuffy Tool®!"

"Last time I checked," stated Becky, "a characteristic of how-to investigate is not a what, and a what is not a how-to respectively. Apparently, the Hoi Polloi thinks nothing of diving straight into the systematic swamp performing a full gainer!"

"There you have it," stated Tom, "the trained mind wallows in swampy ignis fatuus!"

A BURNING DIALECTIC RAGE.

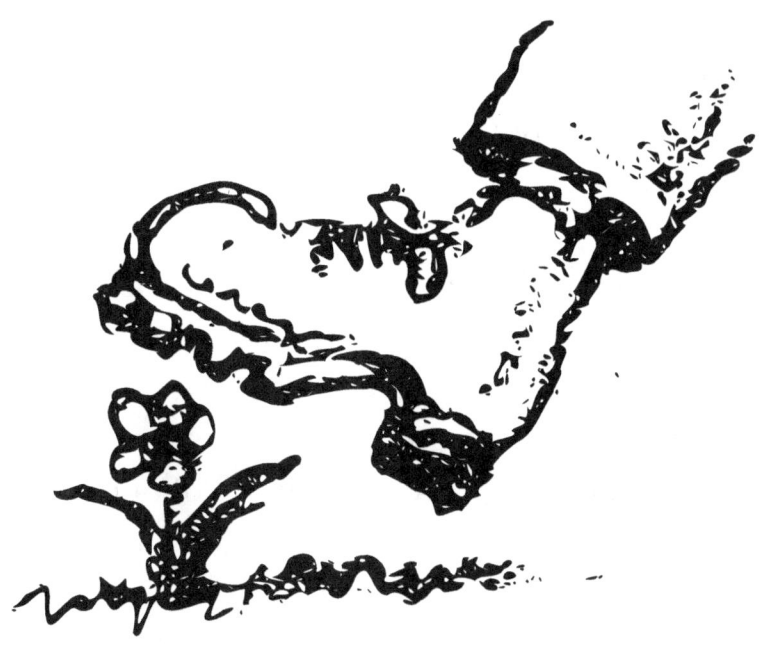

I found Becky's and Tom's recent exchange about art, language, and mind intriguing! I realized how something so obvious, like the lioness expressing language becomes an insurmountable mental challenge for the hypothetically trained mind.

It's actually quite hilarious, or tragic, that a human can't speak its natural born lingo. They trained their mind to speak a bizarro version of said lingo, because it is expedient. Then forgot why they speak the way they do making bizarro compos mentis.

Becky and Tom established that language, history, math and philosophy, were all fish like, that is to say, they were educational and enjoyed by human culture forty thousand years before humans lost their bloody mind and began to blather preposterous hypothetical mythology beyond the five senses.

For example, androgenous Gods and their big fish ideas that can swallow your mind, if you dared to think too much, or monsters deep in the forbidden forest that none have ever seen, but everyone tells frighting stories to prevent the Hoi Polloi from wandering where they are not supposed to be.

Today it's viruses, that none have ever been able to isolate, but everyone parrots the same gruesome myths, because that's the name of academia's game —a hypothetically trained mind preoccupied with bizarro hyperbolic rumors.

The biggest myth of all is that human culture, with its engineering marvels is the byproduct of privatizing the human mind by water-walking Zen masters.

We hear their e-pluribus-unum motto ad nauseam. You know, be a team player, as quantity has a hive-minded quality of its own and that privatization is in our best interest! But what happens when the fish rots from the head, as they always do!

Clearly the only success the hive-mind accomplished was the abasement of the social mind that flourished in spite of their intrigues.

Toward the end of the conversation Becky appeared to get a bit twitchy. Which is understandable, considering the subject matter. After all, who wants to hear that society not only doesn't value your creative efforts, but actively engages in sabotaging them.

Recognizing Becky's agitation, Tom felt speaking more about the creative mind as well as continuing his demolition of the system's self serving myths would prove more progressive.

With that in mind, Tom said to Becky, "We didn't speak about the affect the transformation of the human mind into a Tuffy Tool® has on culture. Specifically, I would like to address your issue with the 'others.'"

"OK," Becky responded, "but like I said, I have my doubts."

"Let's try something different," Tom said, "by turning the world upside down and speak about the mind system to see if that reveals anything."

"For the hypothetical mind," Tom continued, "that is to say, the academically trained accredited mind, meaning is symbolic, because its Third-Language constituents are symbols, and as symbols are part of a system, the Third-Language must have a systematic function, as all systems do."

"Necessarily," stated Becky, "an individual's social function is whatever discipline their mind was trained to perform."

"True," responded Tom. "However, an individual's function does not speak of the system's function."

"Nevertheless," Becky stated, "basic academic training to adequately participate in a technologically cooperative culture is a necessity."

"Well," responded Tom, "considering that our core-tech is constantly under assault by academia, to maintain their hypothetical beguilement, I would ask the question, who is cooperating with whom? Cooperation infers a meeting of minds, not an obligatory indoctrination into a hive-mind system and its harvesting of minds."

"Nevertheless," Tom continued, "that's a self-serving academic myth; that humans can not communicate, cooperate, or technologically advance, unless schooled and managed by an academic."

"We already established language was enjoyed forty millenniums ago," Tom said, "and <u>Dream Duet</u>, situates salient social memories, philosophy, addition, multiplication and even geometry as being firmly established by the metaphorical mind during the Paleolithic period, so we can dismiss another foundational academic myth."

"If language, philosophy, math and geometry are the fruits of the metaphorical mind," stated Becky, "then the academic mind must also be its by-product; albeit crooked as a dog's hind leg."

"It's twisted alright," Tom returned. "Academia has transformed an exciting social process of discovery into a mandatory indoctrination system, sterilized of creative thinking."

"The metaphorical mind," stated Tom, "created an amazing social telescope, then academic loons trained everybody to look out of the wrong damn end!"

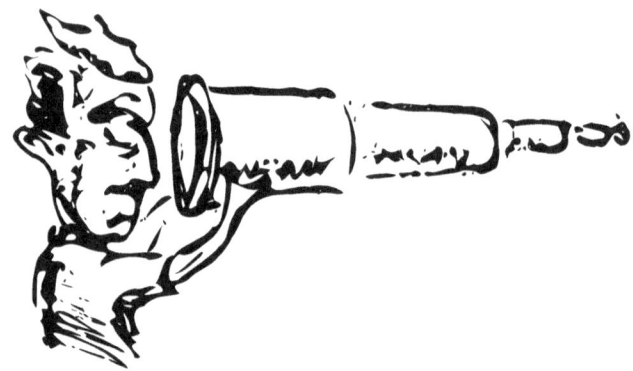

"The question is," Becky asked, "what fundamental systematic function imparts a dead language?"

"Undoubtedly," stated Tom, "we touched on it briefly when we talked about language being striped of imagination and replaced it with the system's logic. Hopefully, the first principle will answer our question in more depth."

"The question is," Becky stated, "how did they plan to accomplish that, that is, the heist of the creative human mind?"

"As Thales is considered the father of academic thought," Tom answered, "because he was the first water-walker to apprehend the supposed fluid evolutionary nature of 'all things,' in an absurd taxonomy predicated on the personification of the human mind's metaphor for philosophy, thus understanding the purpose of Thales deception helps us to understand the Third-Language's function, because it is its by-product."

"Then, when we reexamine Thales' counterfeit bid to school the sovereign metaphorical mind," continued Tom, "Thales didn't personify the rise and setting of the sun. Like his gift bearing ancestors, Thales was attempting to personify the mind's cognitive metaphor, like Artemus personified our awareness of the eternal, or Plato's God personified the Mind-Eternal —language; where the words of our rich legacy were to be 'privatized' and managed by a benevolent water-walking Zen master."

"Apparently," Becky interjected, "the cliché, 'beware of Greeks bearing gifts or free services,' was/is not clearly understood."

"As a mature creative human mind," Tom stipulated, "would never fall for their nonsense, like mistaking the metaphor it uses to express thinking, for what it's thinking about, back in the day when Thales and his ilk were scheming about their mind games, educated Greeks recognized the absurdity and danger of Thales' nonsense, and insisted on a cordon sanitaire. Meaning, Thales was tolerated, so long as he plied his craft exclusively with the Hoi Polloi."

"As such," Tom continued, "the Third-Language, the progeny of Thales' hive-mind system, is a … well … a detached language and mind, untethered from the experiential and its embodied significance, and thus what is real."

"Likewise," Tom continued, "the hive-mind's systematic search for knowledge, is similar to looking for meaning in a sheet of musical symbols. But everyone knows the meaning of music it's not there, it is discovered in the experience of listening to an artist play music."

Becky interjected, "I think you have established the fundamental functional character of the personified Third-Language system. It is a devious hive-mind social process, from which everything is whatever a Sam Hill, water walking, fish hat wearing accreditor like Thales claims!"

"More importantly," Becky said, "I think we have established how they accomplished their palace coup of the creative mind. They take control of language by incremental and small deceptions and with it so goes a piece of the human metaphorical mind, which is an ongoing social process."

"The question is," Tom asked, "what aspect of the human mind is being diminished by their latest sexual assault on metaphorical syntax? What happens to the human mind if it is deliberately misled about the metaphorical meaning of sex, the same way Thales misled them about water; knowing that the female knowledge of any being is non-Cartesian in character?"

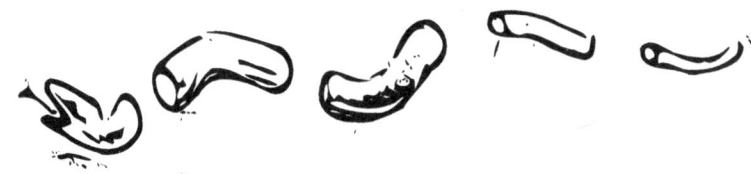

"Obviously," Becky stated, "academia's intention is the same as it ever was, to restrict the Hoi Polloi's ability to Cartesian thinking exclusively, which means the snake will not be able to connect the non-Cartesian metaphorical dots, with a buffoon leading the charge, exclaiming, 'It's the Thing Man, the thing's Thingness —Com'on!'"

"In Occidental culture," Tom said, "the last time the social human mind was sexually assaulted was thousands of years ago to facilitate the transformation from natural metaphorical thinking to a hypothetical system and its hive-mind. That is to say, the transformation from the Second-Language to the Third-Language, which we spoke about extensively with the emergence of a hypothetical species of androgenous Gods."

"Today's sexual assault," Tom stated, "is to facilitate the next transformation from the Third-Language to the Forth-Language, that is, from the hive-mind to AI thinking machines."

"The latest androgynous God that emerged over the last decade," Tom said, "is a real nasty piece of work. To think this God has nothing to do with the current social storm would be naive. It's the last God. It's the technological God of AI, an advocate for human cyborg systems, i.e., thinking machines."

"This is a God that's an existential threat to humanity," Tom claimed, "because it intends to steal our language! Not humans, but their algorithms will censor us, hide the meaning of words and ideas, delete our history, which is our legacy that dates back 40 millenniums, and make all determinations for us, where the human mind will atrophy, like a cashier in a check out line when the power goes down. And art will be considered a heretical practice from a barbaric age, because it's the most ancient social language, a language the AI god can not speak, and thus like Plato, will not permit."

"Notoriously," continued Becky, while speaking in an agitated and animated fashion, "the Hoi Polloi accuse artists of being dreamers, which isn't ironic, or even hypocritical, as both would require their mind to be firmly rooted in the Earth, as opposed to being dead and buried in it."

With her index finger pointing skywards for greater emphasis while shaking it to and fro, Becky stated, "If they threw themselves on the ground, they would likely miss, as their mind was trained to be oblivious to its obliviousness."

"To be candid," Becky confided, "their ad hominem attacks pillorying artists as dreamers is annoying, but what's unnerving is they're as boisterous and obnoxious as Plato in their homilies. Grandma use to always say, 'Loud and slapped plumb stupid, ain't no way to go through life.'"

Sisyphus Slapped Plumb Stupid.

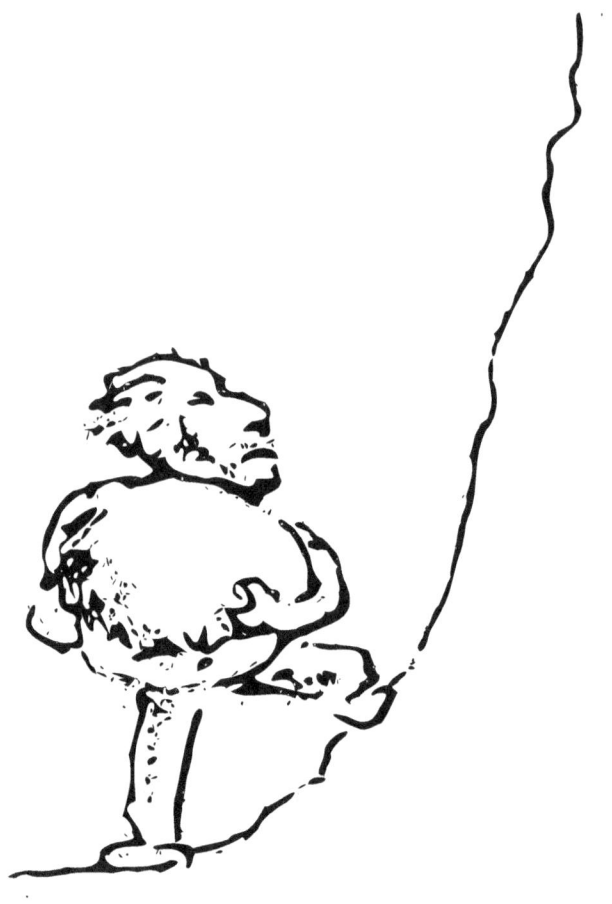

"I noticed when drawing or painting," stated Becky, "during those creative efforts, images appear in my mind's eye. However, when I get distracted, they immediately vanish, in the same way my dreams evaporate when I wake up. By the time I make it to the sink to brush my teeth, I can't make heads or tails of my dream, which just a few steps prior was clear as a bell."

"That's my experience too," Tom said. "The hypothetical mind will not engage our mind's creative way of thinking, for the same reason distractions cause it to vanish. Both of those minds, the hypothetical and distracted minds, are in a behavioral reactive action-mode, as where our creative mind is serenely probative."

"I would have to say," stated Becky, "creative thinking simply requires a wholesome environment that speaks its language and way of doing things, which vanishes when distracted, for whatever reason, which seems to be a natural evolutionary design to deal with challenges that arise."

Tom, leaning forward in his chair appeared to have a vu-jà-dé moment from what Becky just stated.

"That's a subtle and brilliant observation," Tom said, "which explains the reason for the distinction between the minds. It also explains why the hive-mind, is wound way too tight."

"Right," Becky responded, "as we already established, they train the Hoi Polloi's Cartesian mind hypothetically, which makes them oblivious to their metaphorical faculties."

"Moreover," Tom stated, "you also explained the natural function of the Cartesian mind, and why distractions are central in maintaining the Hoi Polloi's beguilement. Like Sisyphus, the academic hive-mind is locked in perpetual action mode, with its pragmatically trained mental processes performing their vain single minded sport in all perpetuity. They can never settle down to achieve the summit of an original thought with their incomplete thinking amid perpetual distractions."

"Even when engaged in so called collective critical-thinking," Tom stated, "they are still running all about, peer reviewing the bugger out of each other, in a confirmation bias."

"Slap yer moma," exclaimed Becky! "That's a perfect, albeit disturbing image of academia's cognitive posture, where flat Earth thinking endures!"

"Thanks," Tom said. "Yet, when we learn to independently develop our metaphorical mind, its probative aspect is not so easily distracted."

"Would you like to rephrase that," asked Becky? "I think the word 'probative' gives the wrong peer reviewing impression!"

"You're right," said Tom, "how about 'imaginative?'"

"Much better," Becky said!

"The academic mind resolving a mathematical equation is not thinking," stated Tom, "because it's cognitively incomplete as it's practical thinking."

"True," stated Becky, "like the Latin phrase, 'ars gratia artis,' if translated to the metaphorically meaningful root level means thinking or imagination must be removed from the context of doing or making. Otherwise it's bias, and thus meaningless."

"Agreed," responded Tom, "You imagine before you draw, in the same way you look before you leap."

"Absolutely, Becky said, "it's the same with how the conscious metaphorical mind builds intellect. The action or doing aspect of the creative process is to determine if our imaginative ideas are feasible. It is the same reason we dream in first (action) and third person (theoretical), that is Cartesian and non-Cartesian thinking; one without the other is incomplete."

"As academia's hypothetical mind training supplants their Delta with the system's logic," Tom stated, "the trained mind has no understanding of the function of the non-Cartesian Delta in the cognitive aspect of the creative process, that is, the learning process."

"Consequently," Tom said, "the trained mind, being oblivious to the Delta, academia builds on the deception by defining the creative process as not having a mental component. Thus, they divide the human mind into two disciplines, science and art where both are reduced to a pragmatic form of doing thinking; that is, memorization and technique."

"Ergo," Becky stated, "when academia defines the creative process, by framing the boundaries of permissible discourse about that which is academia's progenitor, they know damn well they are overstepping their authority."

"Not to mention engaging in hubris beyond measure," mumbled Tom in a Becky like soliloquy.

"Did I say that aloud," asked Tom coyly?

"You sure did," responded Becky. "However, you stopped just shy of accusing academia of having an Oedipus complex with a burning dialectic rage to first murder then shag its metaphorical maker in a twisted necrophiliac fantasy."

"I didn't say that," exclaimed Tom, while the white of his eyes grew!

"Yea, but I could hear you thinking it," returned Becky, while laughing.

TREAT'EM LIKE SHROOMS!

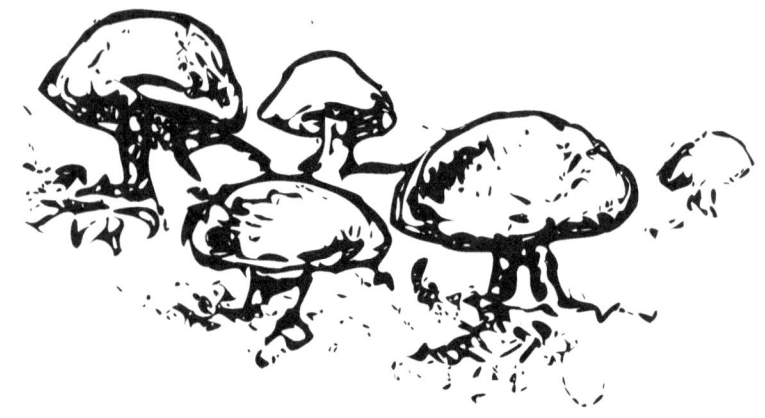

Compared to when the conversation began, when Becky was obviously vexed as her ideas were replete with soliloquies and double analogies, I was glad to see she regained her spirit, even though her issue with the 'others' was no closer to being resolved.

It appeared that Becky was developing a clearer understanding that she was not strictly speaking with a human being, and began to rethink her approach about how to interact with a hybrid.

In a very real sense, both a hybrid channeling the system and an AI thinking machine are very similar in that regard; they are both programmed in a dead hypothetical Third-Language, which precludes them from metaphorical thinking on the root level. It's common sense, a machine or mind trained to think in a systematic level language, can not understand or speak in the base language without a compiler.

They can mouth the words, but they are without meaning or any understanding and thus can not inspire. And as Tom stated, "artists do not speak 'words,' they are in the business of forming new 'words' on the root level," likewise, when academia speaks about creativity or pretends that their AI machines can be imaginative, they are simply doing what they have been doing for thousand of years since the time of the pre-Socratics … mucking about in the Delta.

That also tells us, they will never stop attacking the Delta and will use every means at their disposal. And when we consider the tech available to water-walkers today, I think Becky's idea of opening a dialogue with the Hoi Polloi is very circumspect.

"We didn't quite resolve the issue of opening a dialogue with the 'others,'" stated Becky. "Apparently, the process is like trying to take a dog's bone. The closer we get, the more illusive it becomes."

"My gut instinct tells me," Tom said, "it's not exclusively a language problem."

"Agreed," stated Becky. "I don't think a simple translation will breach their walls. Their hive-mind conditioning makes them unreceptive, even hostile to ideas that contradicts their mind training. And how does one translate from a living to a dead language, or communicate with a Cartesian mind locked in behavioral mode?"

"You're right," responded Tom.

"As it stands," Becky continued, "the hive-mind is restricted to a pragmatic form of doing-thinking, which requires repetitive training in mental techniques for decades. That tells us the 'others' are trained to memorize –not comprehend, to believe –not investigate, to react –not think."

"I do know one thing with absolute certainty," Tom stated. "I would rather have a tooth extracted than argue with a hybrid. You will have to deconstruct their hypothesis to identify every hypothesis it is built on, then repeat the process for each subsequent hypothesis, until you drill down generationally to the root level for them all, each of which you will find is built on century old opinions of some water walking idiot. Yet, even if you were able to flush out those Augean Stables, that won't make them any less arrogant or more receptive to your creative ideas."

"Actually," Becky said, "all you have to do is undermine one hypothetical and their hypothesis withers and dries-up."

"Right," Tom stated. "However, when you chase one hypothetical down, you quickly find they are descendants in an inbred family tree. And if you dig a little deeper, you will discover everything boils down to phenomenology on the metaphorical base level with its fundamental tenets like sameness, differentness, allness, thingness, and so on and so forth, all of which are paradoxical in nature. Yet, every subsequent idea like our sense of the eternal springs from them."

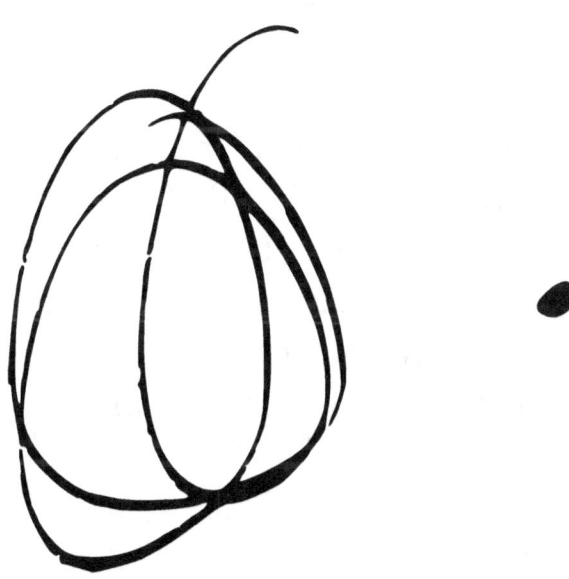

"Right," interjected Becky, "no one has ever actually bumped into a sameness to definitively establish its veracity. And as we have established, the hybrid can not think on the base level, when they use mathematics beyond practical applications to prove their hypothetical idea, how does one break the news to them that math, or thingness if you will, is paradoxical and thus it's not proof of anything."

"I mean come on," Becky stated, "if I give the same statistical values to ten individuals, I get ten different opinions. And if I give the raw numbers to those same individuals, I get ten different statistical sets of values. I would recommend academics read Zeno's dichotomy paradox to get their hypothetical mind right."

"Respectively," stated Tom, "that makes arguing with a hybrid, a moot point. Both sides of their equation may be congruent, but for the metaphorical language and mind, the meaning of things and the truth, whatever the hell that is, are more enigmatic than congruency, which makes the trained mind go tits-up."

"That's picturesque," interjected Becky!

"Thanks," stated Tom, "and as we have metaphorically established all beings are domains of knowledge, like the sky being is knowledge of the overview, that means any being's knowledge is by nature relative to their environment, which explains why the Hoi Polloi's language and mind has socially evolved into a hypothetical simulacrum."

"Hybrid's speak the language of the technological construct in which they dwell," stated Tom. "Add academia's mind games, Hollywood's nonsense, and antisocial-media to their abode and their mind orbits the outer limits of Wonder-World with no umbilicus!"

"The hybrid's mind is incompatible with the creative mind," Tom stated, "because they think in a dead language and their mind is locked in behavioral mode. We have nothing in common. The trained mind's symbols hold no metaphorical semantic meaning, and its syntax has no import with the Delta's living logic."

"OK," stated Becky, "so we have finally established why the Hoi Polloi don't understand artists. But, we are no closer to opening a dialogue."

"They may have lost their proverbial mind to tech," Tom suggested. "However, the hybrid's physical being did not evolve from its artificial environment. It is a socio-technological aboutness if you will. Separate them from their tech, and we can still reach them on a non-Cartesian level."

"Right," Becky said, "and as you suggested previously, art is the only way to penetrate their thick skulls, as the metaphorical is their Achilles' heel, which is why Plato attacked the arts, which then establishes academia's hypothetical mind training rests on duplicity."

"Henceforth, Becky proclaimed, with her finger pointing skyward again, "I will treat the Hoi Polloi like mushrooms, keep them in the dark and dine them on hors d'oeuvre de la ordure, followed by a fresh steaming pile as the main course!"

"Obviously," Tom said laughing, while trying to put his drink down so as not to spill it, "as frustrating as it is for an artist, you can not speak to the 'others' the way you speak to me, and if you do they will always react the same way. As we already established, a higher level language can't speak the base language."

"Nevertheless," Tom said, "we can answer their questions with a degree of sincerity. Yet, if we couch metaphorical ideas in hypothetical terms, that's where we get into trouble. We have to stop dumbing down our metaphorical ideas. Let them go cockeyed!"

"However, when we do speak to the Hoi Polloi on a base level," Tom stipulated, "we have to speak, not in a dumb down manner, but metaphorically infantile, because they never developed their natural mind. Which is what academia does, they attack the Delta on the most infantile way, i.e. the obliteration of the female gender."

"I understand," Becky said, with a hang-dog look. "Thus they may only be able to catch a glimpse of what we are saying in a peripheral manner."

"I think so," Tom said. "That explains why they view art as mysterious. They are moved by what we do, even inspired by it; unlike academia's metaphorical assaults that engenders disenchantment, despondency and hopelessness."

"Moreover," Tom stated, "when a hybrid catches a glimpse of their natural mind from your art, they become inspired and want to know more about creativity, and when they imagine ways that deliberately blur the boundary between those doing and speculative domains, that's when the two minds begin to interact in musical harmony, instead of the constant bickering they hear, like the annoying dissonant noise between academia and the arts."

"Subsequently," Tom said, "a hybrid may feel like Rip Van Winkle, hypothetically slumbering for their entire lives, that suddenly 'woke!'"

Shangri-la's Pro Tempore Ad-hoc Rules.

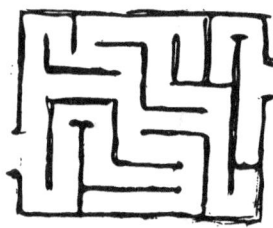

"Lord please help me over the fence," shouted Becky! "Your usage of the word 'woke' disrupted my calm and put my mind in immediate reactive action mode."

"It reminded me of those adrift at sea etymological zealots of academia, with their incessant proselytizing sermons about the deep pedantic importance of non-binary pronouns," Becky added.

"Ahh …," stated Tom, "the language canard — academia's stock in trade. Apparently, they want us to believe their trained high school prodigies, who can barely read, write and count, are venerated Zen masters of linguistic anthropology, without a clue as to what language actually is, all the while they are channeling the non-binary spirits of Greek oligarchs and their wet-dream of drowning the creative human mind's actual metaphorical language in its own Delta."

"Obviously," Becky said, "academia is stirring the pot —agitating everyone."

"When was the last time you created a work of art, when some pencil neck geek pissed-on ya and told you it was raining," asked Becky?"

"Well …," stated Tom. … I ahh …

"That's what I thought," interrupted Becky. "It's impossible —you taught me that."

"Thank you," said Tom, "but, what I was going to say is, academia is extremely devious in their assaults against the creative human mind. Their latest non-binary campaign, crafted to obliterate the human mind's awareness of its sexual syntax went something like the following:"

"Academia sold the Hoi Polloi a hypothetical bill of goods," said Tom, "about a remarkable vision of a virtual Shangri-la, teaming with enlightened beings, where all boats could rise and visit distant shores."

"That sounds wonderful," interjected Becky, with one eyebrow raised, knowing Tom was about to drop the anchor.

"However," Tom pointed out, "the Hoi Polloi, oblivious to academia's ideological training of an entire generation of entomological zealots, were unwitting participants in the color revolution being amassed against the creative human mind."

"Next," continued Tom, "was academia's poison-pill to protect their undertaking. They convinced the unwitting Hoi Polloi that their virtual Shangri-la required a series of temporary ad hoc rules and technological instruments to restrict virtual free speech, on the pretext of protecting their children from perverts."

"Being oblivious to the former plans," stated Tom, "and now the latter's outrageous contradiction, because of their hive-minded behavioral conditioning, the Hoi Polloi obediently complied and help facilitate every measure being leveed against them."

"Then when academia launched their Delta campaign," Tom pointed out, "which mis-gendered their children and exposed them to the same perverts those regulations were supposed to protect them from, academic ideologues pirouetted the instruments crafted to protect children from perverts against any objectionable free speech."

"Sanctimoniously," added Becky, "to further confound the Hoi Polloi's sensibilities, academia butchered the definition of female in every virtual nook and cranny, while promoting advertising campaigns to resurrect Descartes' epistemological doubts from the great beyond!"

"Consequentially," Tom said, "as the Hoi Polloi is dependent on academia, because of their hive-mind behavioral conditioning, which was now in opposition with their ability to perceive and instinct to protect their children, that resulted in cognitive dissonance and social discord, which academia's trained ideologues reeked havoc from below, while academia managed the circus from above."

"Predictably," stated Becky, "during the pedantic carnival, while everyone was engaged in polemics over the multitude of new genders breeding like rabbits in the virtual-sphere, the Hoi Polloi was oblivious to the palace coup underway in the creative-sphere, i.e., the assault on their sovereign metaphorical mind."

"Ergo,' Becky added, "it was a multifaceted stratagem involving high minded buffoons, the demolition of our syntactical metaphor, the abolition of free speech, training a generation of crass ideologues, socially facilitating mass cognitive dissonance, and last but not least academia obliterated Shangri-la —sinking all boats to Davy Jones' locker."

"Even in a lawless nation," Tom stated, "metaphorical imagination is not open for academic peer review. That's why academia's linguistic assaults, which always strike at the metaphorical root, are shrewdly crafted ruses, rumored to be of grass-root origin in some ideological social movement, which academia's gung ho zealots faithfully parrot."

"However," continued Tom, "everyone knows that grass-root rebellions by the Hoi Polloi never happened in the history of civilization. Rebellions always travel downward from above."

"Agreed," Becky interjected, "as do most judicious chroniclers with any sand. And as we have already established, the personified first principle of their collective hive mind training prevents the Hoi Polloi from thinking independently, that precludes them from rebelling."

"The question is," Becky said, "why is academia assaulting the metaphorical mind at this particular juncture, and cui bono?"

"Well, … " Tom said, "You answered your own question. Academia had to degrade Shangri-la into a fool's paradise, because too many of the Hoi Polloi were starting to emerge from their hypothetical slumber and could potentially discover their creative potential."

"Similar to the age of the Gutenberg Press," Tom stated, "the payoff during the age of the Internet, is the same as it ever was, to maintain their systematic siege of the social construct, i.e., the Mind-Eternal, and thus control of the human mind and its will."

"It's an eternal battle," stated Tom, "between orthodoxy and heterodoxy, that is, academia and the arts, or between the hive and creative mind, if you will."

"A social Shangri-la," Tom stated, "has the real potential of one day facilitating a cognitive social Renaissance."

"Well," Becky stated, "that Renaissance is obviously not today, considering the level of cognitive dissonance pervasive in Shangri-la turned pell-mell."

"However," said Tom, "in such a dubious culture, we can't trust anything virtual, be it Internet, TV, radio, print, or even their hypothetical language. Yet, on a brighter note, the scope of their colossal efforts against the creative mind tells us they lost control of the hive-mind."

"Typically," Becky said, "like the barbaric cancel-culture of the Church during the age of Gutenberg Press, which was the academy of that day, academia during the age of the Internet devolved back into the crusading religious institutional proclivities of their Dark Age predecessors."

"That's what academia does," Tom said, "when we begin awakening, they ramp up their beguilement, and when that doesn't work they bring back the good old Dark Ages of cancel-culture barbecues, shunnings, banishments, firings, unfriendings, de-platformings, fact checkings, and so on and so forth!"

"Obviously," Becky said, "academia dropped the Enlightenment from their curriculum."

The Immaculate Conception of Flickers.

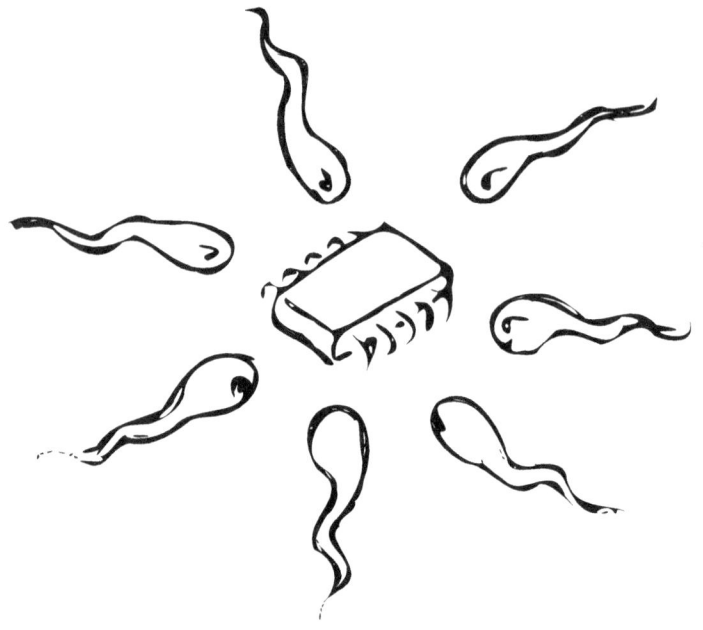

Excitedly, Becky stood up and stated, "I just realized how it's possible to open a dialogue with the 'others' from what we have just discussed; aside from letting my art do all of the talking."

"There are two things we have to consider prior to reaching the implacable mind," Becky said. "The first has to do with damage assessment, and the second relates to the environment."

"I think it primarily comes down to a question of how much hypothetical injury their minds received," concluded Becky. "I mean someone with a PhD and their disciples, forget about them. Their minds are buried under mountainous layers of hypothetical sediment. Therefore, it's the young ones that may be receptive."

"However," Becky stipulated while retaking her seat, "as teens are easily distracted, and knowing a tranquil space is essential for creative thinking to flourish, that makes the environment central, but also problematic. It's not a pretty sight prying an adolescent away from their synthetically distributed hive-minds!"

"I think you're heading in the right direction," Tom said. "We can't reach a mind distracted with incessant cell phone alerts, or immersed in hypothetical hallucinations. Their mind gets easily confused between hypothetical conjecture and reality."

"As we previously established," Tom said, "the distinction between the behavior oriented pragmatic mind and its imaginative counterpart, determines if the mind is being reactive or probative —respectively, and as the hypothetical mind substitutes behavioral mind conditioning for probative speculation, like everything else they do, their mind's function is inverted."

"Ergo," Tom said, "the hypothetically trained mind, is in constant turmoil; flickering between different functional uses of cognitive pathways, causing them to hypothetically hallucinate."

"Likewise," continued Becky, "when they are not being distracted, they're all out picking hypothetical posies, in some sort of virtual signaling, peer reviewing support group. I am surprised they can walk a straight line while flickering!"

"Well … ," returned Tom, "academics are not known for their athletic prowess."

"The hypothetical hallucinations of the trained mind," Tom continued, "can be recognized when I speak about the Third-Language as being a system, because that's not the full verity of the matter. It's more of an expression of their trained mind's character."

"A language system is not language," Tom stated, "language is language, or I should say it is languaging. Languaging can not be a system any more than a system can be anything. The word system is simply speaking about the functional use of a thing, be it language, transportation, or whatever. They are hypothetical things, which is magical thinking. Like that hypothetical table you set your drink on a while back."

"Now hold on Tom," interjected Becky, who sat up in her chair with indignation and stated, "I was not flickering. I lost control, because of what you said, in the same way you mistook me for a back-splash when you gave me that Chardonnay shower."

"All right, my mistake," admitted Tom. "I'm just saying, if I train a mind for decades to exclusively speak and think with the symbols and the logic of a personified hypothetical system, knowing full well that systems are the utilitarian illusions of a hybrid's mind, for such an unnaturally trained mind, like Plato's yahoos in his <u>Allegory of the Cave</u>, metaphorical reality will be a serious challenge."

"The only way a system can become a thing," Tom said, "is if their simulacrum has a non-binary immaculate conception, like language. I have seen someone languaging, but I have never actually seen a language, because it's not a thing, it's what the mind does; artists call it imagination and its metaphorical expressions."

"That makes sense," Becky said. "However, to a flicker, who can't find the Northern end of a South bound polecat, they won't understand. I mean how does one break the bad news to a flicker that they are the being that hallucinates? They'll immediately go cockeyed, then get agitated, followed by an ad hominem serenade."

"Without access to their Delta and its mind of the ages, their only recourse to know what is or is not real," said Tom, "is to ask a flickering academic genius sitting in a ditch teaming with lemmings."

"Let me see if I can state that hilarious predicament in my burgeoning Southern way of speaking," stated Tom, with great enthusiasm.

"Jesus wept Tom, when you do that, you make me lose my Religion," exclaimed Becky!

By the way, discouraging Tom was Becky's way of encouraging him. You know, attempting to stop someone from doing something is the surest way to achieve the opposite.

Predictably, Tom ignored her and proceeded to preform his best oratorical effort in Becky-Speak:

"As there is already a congregation in the ditch, each of which are trepidatiously grasping a fist full of daffodils," Tom began while grinning, "others suss out, that must be the best way to go, and proceed to jump straight into yonder ditch; birds of a feather and all that. However, when I squawk at them, suggesting that they are wallowing in the mud, they look at me as if I lack the good sense that God gave a goose!"

As expected, Becky heaped on more discouragement. "Your Southern needs a lot of work Tom. You've got the right ah-ha, but the wrong ça-va," concluded Becky in a resolute tone!"

"What the hell does that mean," Tom exclaimed puzzled? "Never mind," mumbled Tom in a disenchanted tone, who perfunctorily returned to his native dialect.

"When the system selects a blithering idiot for the highest political office," stated Tom, "what the oligarchs are training their Tuffy Tools® to accept is, an academic's ideas are as incidental to the academic system, as a politician's are to the political system, or any other social system. Biden conveys that sentiment par excellence with his mindless gaffs, 'It's the Thing, Man!'"

"The reason is obvious," stated Becky. "They are transitioning our social systems to their AI algorithms which makes democratic participation obsolete."

Tom, being the determined type, although he dropped his feeble attempt at speaking Southern, he did perform a Becky soliloquy to get a rise out of her. Tom reenacted Becky's literary device as if speaking to an imaginary Biden that was behind him:

"No Jo-Jo, it's not called a thing, it's called a system that ships us off to system-school to get our minds pruned," stated Tom while speaking over his shoulder to the incorporeal Jo-Jo. "Com'on MAN, you should know that. We are being sent to useful school, so we too can drive our minds straight into a ditch."

Becky was as amused at Tom mimicking her as she was about the subject of his performance. "I like it better when you speak sincerely," stated Becky, "because you're brutal. Your thinking makes people question their sanity more than Jo-Jo's!"

First Principle & Reverse Biden Effect.

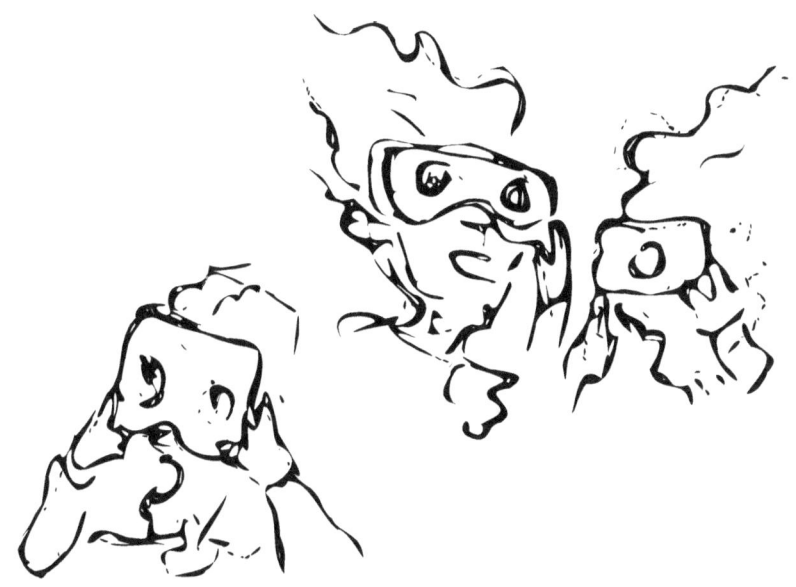

"It's not as bad as all that," suggested Tom. "We just have to think more on the root level. As happened previously in our history during a period very similar to today called the Renaissance. Like then, no amount of academic vandalism in the Delta can possibility beguile the creative human mind."

"Einstein understood that, Tom said. "He was asked, how he was able to think of such creative ideas, and his answer was simple, instead of thinking academically he used his imagination like Cézanne. It's creative ideas that determine our destiny, because they inspire, and nothing can stop the reawakening of the human mind any more than they can prevent the reemergence of life in springtime."

"I've been doing that my entire life," claimed Becky. "Yet, I was never really cognizant of the mental process, any more than I am aware of my beating heart, unless I'm running at break-neck speed, … which appears to be what you are doing with your mind. Aren't you worried you will blow a mental pathway and go plumb crazy," asked Becky?

"Not a chance," answered Tom. "It's the flickering hypothetical mind that is revving their pathways at unnaturally dangerous levels. I don't even have to touch the throttle, because I'm not fighting the Delta's current, I'm going with its flow~"

"Nevertheless," continued Becky, "I am curious. I want to hear more about your understanding of how the process works, even though it may screw me up for life!"

"Glad to hep," quipped Tom, while avoiding eye contact.

"The first principle is always the best place to begin," Tom surmised. "If I was a machine, I would naturally only understand 0's and 1's, which for us mortals is the metaphorical; that is, human-machine-code."

"However," Tom added, "as both the metaphorical, as well as 0's and 1's, are systematically difficult to debug, the system trains the Hoi Polloi's mind to only understand at its systematic level, like C++, but without a compiler. Hence, the disconnect between mind and world."

"If I'm following you correctly," Becky stated, "getting out of the ditch, is as much a process of unlearning —not what we learned —but how we were trained to learn, as well as listening to how our mind naturally investigates."

"I would think so," returned Tom, "with the caveat of making a clear distinction between memorized systematic trivium, and conceptual knowledge that was metaphorically cultivated."

"Also," Becky interjected, "in the way I misconstrued the snake metaphor as a symbol for language, we have to be vigilant in distinguishing between natural cognitive processes and behavioral conditioning."

"That's true, but not too difficult," Tom suggested. "Obviously, being aware of the problem is half the battle. It's also important to not be compulsive, being patient and not rushing to judgment."

"Comparing an idea in question with metaphorically established ideas is also circumspect," Becky said.

"Additionally," Tom advised, "If you find yourself thinking too much, you likely have a problem. Because the metaphorical mind, as complex as its ideas can be, metaphorical thinking comes to us effortlessly."

"Moreover," interjected Becky, "the most effective method is to ensure our environment is free from distractions."

"Absolutely," Tom said, "For me that process is about listening to how my mind is designed to think, as much as it's about my passionate question, because how it thinks is syntactical. Basically, I let it off of it's leash and just let it play, and stop thinking about how I should think."

"Interesting," stated Becky, "let it do its thing. Yet, artwork, or the doing aspect of art-making, is definitely a social process."

"Unquestionably," Becky said, "the participation of the 'others' engaging in the doing aspect of the process can range from being spectators to active collaborators."

"However," Tom stated, "as we are well aware, that conversation is problematic at best, thus when socially engaging, artists must take into account the overbearing academic zeitgeist we need to surmount."

"Yea," stated Becky, "I'm going to carve them in stone like the ten commandments, and at the top of the list will be, 'Thou shalt not hypothetically hallucinate!'"

"Great idea," said Tom. "Give me a copy for my living room wall. I have one you can add, 'Thou shalt not spend a penny in thine Delta!'"

"We can save that project for another chat," Becky said.

"Good," Tom replied, "sounds like it will be fun."

"Additionally," Tom pointed out, "stereotypes about what art is, like highly polished technical works, could be abandoned for more honest, or child like expressions, which will have the effect of undermining prosaic beliefs about what art is, and open the door to art-making to everyone. I would call it the reverse Biden effect."

"What in Sam Hill is the reverse Biden effect," asked Becky, with a dotty look?

"You know … It's the opposite of the Biden effect," Tom stipulated, while grinning.

"Biden," stated Tom, "being a professionally dressed, well groomed, entourage attended, red carpet perambulating tribune, whose veto power over the Senate affects millions of lives, and is thus incessantly stalked by a swarm of paparazzi, stringers and newshounds, all anticipating some profound words of wisdom from the occupant of the Hoi Polloi's most revered office, like a herd of hungry horses anticipating molasses flavored oats for dinner —yet, any question they pose more Herculean than Biden's preferred flavor of ice-cream, the bungling tribune is about as cogent as a frustrated tongue-tied-toddler vocalizing cacophonies!"

"Obviously," Becky stated while laughing, "the reverse Biden effect in art-making, would be to communicate profound thinking in a child like manner, which would overcome most previously mentioned obstacles that undermines the social aspect of art making. Well done Tom. I owe you a box of crayons, because that's the closest we have ever gotten to opening a dialogue with the 'others!'"

Tom's eyebrow raised at the crayon reward, as he stated, "We're just inverting the Biden effect. Both are incongruent social identities crafted to throw someone off balance, like a scruffy snot nosed toddler playing Mozart, or a crass know-it-all teen lecturing us about non-binary linguistic anthropology. It's mental Judo, used to create cognitive dissonance."

"Getting back to the seminal aspect of creative endeavors," Tom said, "which most are trained to believe to be some sort of esoteric bodily function, that needs to be expressed by a primitive creature beyond the purview of genteel sensibility, we need to add another caveat."

"Specifically," Tom stipulated, "reaching out to 'others' for their opinion on the matter, whatever it may be, especially an academic's, will close all locks between waterways. You will never gain access to your mind, unless you dive in and learn to swim for yourself, which is the first syntactical device of reclaiming authorship of your mind and thus resuming your sovereign status as master and commander of the Delta's Bounding-Main!"

"That's where that pirate Thales gets to walk the plank, at the tip of your cutlass," interjected Becky.

"Unfortunately," returned Tom, "with a lifetime of hypothetical mind injury, Thales is not that easily jettisoned to Davy Jones' locker."

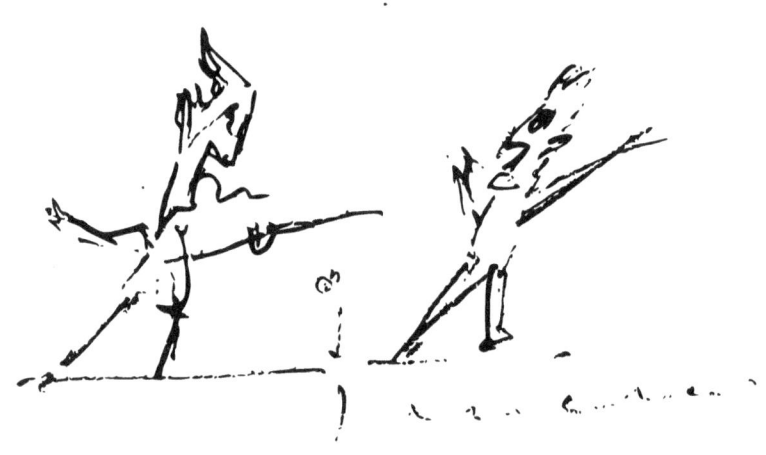

"Nevertheless," Tom continued, "I recommend we trust our amazing capacity first and foremost, then and only then reach out to the 'others', that just so happen to be sitting in a ditch."

"What's the point," asked Becky?

"Exactly," returned Tom, "and by the way, I want a big box of crayons, not the silly small set of primary and secondary colors! I want a box with aquamarine and cobalt blue."

"I'll get right on that Tom," returned Becky.

At this point in Becky's and Tom's conversation, I was taken a step back, because their challenge with academia is as fundamental as humanism's was with the academy of the Medieval period, i.e., the Church.

However, Becky and Tom clearly establish a cogent solution to mitigate the precarious mental state of the hypothetically trained mind —the compiler, which is not unreasonable. In fact, it's warranted, considering the Zen water walking personified first principle of their so called rationale, as well as academia's hypocritical, dare I say criminal linguistic assaults against the Delta, which violate their lofty mandate and fiduciary duty.

However, after listening to Becky's and Tom's continued exchange about when the Renaissance will occur, the word imminent does not describe their forecast ...

The Rumpus Over a Missing Compiler.

"When I impart that bit of insight to an academic," Tom stated, "that is, your logic is missing a compiler, said academic, who is ordinarily as calm as the glass like stillness of an undisturbed pond at sunrise, becomes unstable."

"A circus ordinarily commences," Tom declared. "It begins with the same wandering gaze at the ceiling, except their mouth is agape accompanied with a squinted brow. Which tells me they are trying to determine if I just called them an idiot!"

"It becomes apparent they have made their determination," said Tom, "when their mouth shuts tighter than a frog's proverbial."

While smiling, Becky interjected, "I know that pejorative glare. I have seen it many times by the academic know-it-all that thinks the sun comes up just to hear them crow. It warms my heart you left them speechless, which is no easy task."

"It gets more exciting," Tom said. "At that point in time one of three things often occur. The first is laughter, and we continue exchanging idiotic ideas, which happens once in a blue moon. The second is they walk away in a huff, or the third option is, a cabaret unfolds!"

"I personally prefer laughter," Tom stated, "while my next choice is the cabaret, because the indignant ones are precarious. They often return later when you least expect. And as their mind's are built like a Swiss watch, and knowing I will not have time to unwind their hypothetical Gordian knot, when I see their wild eyed hungry look and salivating step upon returning, I forestall the encounter, which makes the precarious ones rabid!"

"As such," Tom said, "in my tactical retreat, as I am walking away ever so cautiously, while they are nipping at my heals, I do listen intently to their earsplitting histrionics, so when I encounter them later, after having ample time to sift through their embroiling hokum, I can step on their tail!"

"The last time I witnessed an academic having a dying duck fit, was in 4th grade after the back of Mr. Harding's bald head was pelted with spit balls," quipped Becky.

"Oh … the good old days," Tom said while smiling. "I too have fond memories of punctuating Ms. Tenderbottom's you know what, that and her blackboard algebraic calculations, with real juicy spit-wads —to make damn sure they stuck. You can guess which target sent the academic decorum straight into the crapper. It was very educational!"

Following that childish exchange that continued for some time, Tom said, "I certainly understand why they lose their footing. The implications are profound, holding individual, social, as well as historical significance. But there is much more at stake then academia's credibility, or an academic's career."

"As a master artist," continued Tom, "my loyalty lays with the bridge builders that painted the cave of Chauvet in France, which was/is the original blueprint for the social mind."

"And to be abundantly clear with the hive-mind that hypothetically hypothesizes," said Tom, "we have to resolutely state, we are not being meta-metaphorical. Otherwise, they will presume we are saying that expressive colorful hand-prints and scribbles are early forms of language."

"No," declared Tom resolutely! "Chauvet was built by social architects that were masters of the human mind. Chauvet is the first story. It's the greatest story ever told. It's the story of the birth of the Mind-Eternal!"

"Absolutely," Becky stated. "However, as we have previously established, the core-tech is not Cro-Academia's, that revelation will instantly burst a Cro-Academic's tail into spontaneous combustion, for the same reason the assertion that their language is missing its compiler."

"Both ideas," Tom agreed, "dispatch their minds to absolute Bedlam. Because it strikes at the root of their social function; that maybe, after millenniums of thinking themselves and their disciples straight into one ditch after another, they really don't know what the hell they are talking about, and that they may not be the brightest bulbs on the tree after all!"

THE ACTUAL BIG BADA BOOM*

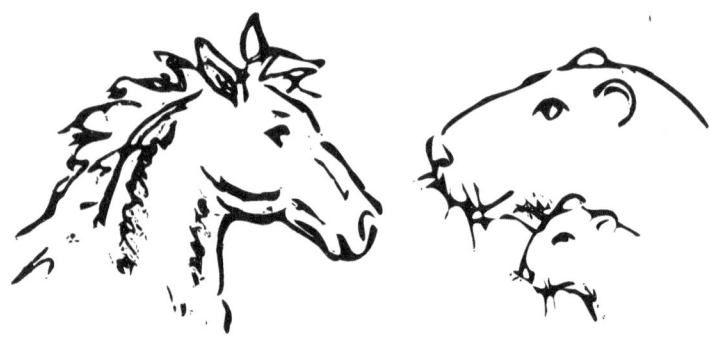

I think Becky and Tom came to the inevitable conclusion that the law of unintended consequences reigns supreme.

Humans created mind-tech that extended the mortal reach of the human mind socially that could now speak in terms of millenniums. Unfortunately, they left their collective mind-tech vulnerable to predators, who then claimed ownership of it, then proceeded to transform their language and mind into a Tuffy Tool®, which subsequently rendered them so screwed-up they are now incapable of understanding human language, which means they don't know who the hell they are.

Circumspectly, Becky and Tom talked less about how to communicate with a hybrid nutter, and more about how to extricate themselves from academia's ditches. But more importantly, how not to drive into them to begin with.

Humorously, Becky and Tom entertained the possibility of using the same mental judo academia uses against the Delta to awaken their hallucinating flickers.

On a brighter, yet bitter sweet note, the fact that today's global syndicate of mind managers are waging a vicious global war against the Delta, Becky and Tom understood there are a lot more Hoi Polloi waking up from their hypothetical slumber!

I think Becky and Tom clearly understood that, because their attitude became noticeably upbeat, dare I say, optimistic!

"Bang", declared Tom! "That was the actual big bada boom that set 'all things' in motion, which most certainly had nothing to do with a howling, flaming tailed academic. It was Neanderthal's mind-tech at Chauvet that stirred up a social storm in the Delta!"

"Which, Tom said, "aside from all of the aforementioned reasons as to why Cro-Academics and their side kicks are missing their compiler, the fact that the mind-tech is not theirs, offers us an additional explanation as to why the hybrid's mind was Humpty Dumped."

"Being eclectic," Tom continued, "and thus having understood just enough to recognize the mind-tech was useful, they trained their mind with another species mind-tech, while being oblivious of the profound debilitating effect that would have on their intellect."

"That's not how the creative mind functions, stated Becky. "Its intellect is built from life, not mind-tech. As usual, they have the cart before the horse."

"True," Tom returned, "and as we all know, tech, being one of those gifts that keeps on giving, there is always a price to be paid, as Spencer Tracy so eloquently performed that sentiment in the movie, <u>Inherit The Wind</u>, '… I think there's a man who sits behind a counter and says, All right, … Mister, you may conquer the air, but the birds will lose their wonder, and the clouds will smell of gasoline!'"

"I found that movie one sided," said Becky. "The antagonistic characters were way over modeled, almost cartoonish. However, I suppose that's the way to establish your position, while not giving the opposing counsel any rope."

"I agree," returned Tom, "and that's academia's animated position as well. As our mind training destroys any possibility of formulating a meaningful defense in their personified trial of 'all things,' just like the director's point of view in that movie, only academia's voice is socially argued."

"Also," Becky stated, "like the cartoonish characters in that movie, it's the trained and supposedly enlightened mind that's intolerant. It's incapable of dialogue. It can only engage in argument, which is an inevitable consequence of their behavioral mind conditioning."

"Which," Tom pointed out, "is why conversing with a trained mind, the act of listening becomes a tactic; a passive-aggressive maneuver in defense of their mind training, like a lawyer or liar, all of which are distinctions without a difference."

"Moreover," Becky added, "if the hybrid finds it's in unfamiliar intellectual territory, beyond its training, which is a forgone conclusion when conversing with yours truly, their behaviorally trained mind, which is naturally designed to instinctively react emotionally when threatened, which includes anyone who thinks differently, they engage in strange psychological behavior."

"As you previously established," Tom said, "unless we separate them from their tech and facilitate a tranquil space that transports the trained mind to their happy place, which is essential for creative thinking to emerge, communicating with a hybrid is problematic."

"Consequently," Tom explained, "the price of using the mind-tech of another species with no understanding of what it was and how it would affect the human mind, may have been expedient, but, their actions were as careless then, as their hypothetical thinking is meaningless today."

"Likewise," Tom continued, "their beguiling definition of ancient art and the human mind is used as justification for every generation's mind training, with the same damn meaningless core-tech."

"Which is a lot like grandma's nightie," stated Tom, "it covers everything, thank you very much. Yet, if we dare venture a peek under the gown … well … suffice it to say, nothing piques our interest."

"Leave our beloved grandmas out of this sordid affair," interrupted Becky! "Verily, your idea of taking a look-see under grandma's gown has conjured up an array of disturbing images, I won't be able to unsee!"

"Your right, I apologize. I crossed the line," Tom said. "I couldn't help myself. I too love my Grandma, bless her bow legged heart."

Both busted out in laughter, and following that childish exchange, Tom and Becky continued their conversation about the precarious mental state of the eclectic mind and its systematic behavioral conditioning.

"Unlike the hypothetical Third-Language," said Tom, "which requires a living being to train another in its use, the living metaphorical ideas of Chauvet can be shared across oceans of time without any mind training, because it requires one thing only to comprehend what was expressed; an understanding of how the natural human mind negotiates the navigation of its world."

"Is that the mysterious missing compiler you keep mentioning," asked Becky?

"Yes, it is," returned Tom, "which makes sense, if we think of our mind as a musical instrument. Without knowing how the instrument works, we are unable to explore its subtleties, and thus we're simply playing our mind in the same way a toddler would play the piano —with their fists and feet."

"Ergo," Becky exclaimed, "the big bada boom!"

"Obviously," concluded Tom, "there can only be one response to such hokum, 'As an artist, who has studied what is meaningful, and thus what is real, should I not be asking a Cro-Academic, whose collective personified mind perceives whatever hypothetical thing they so desire, from what meaningful ground do you make such a wild claim, and by what authority do you presume to school the sovereign metaphorical mind with such malpractice?'"

"Very circumspect," stated Becky. "However, charging academia for having a bonehead idea, is like accusing a bureaucrat of duplicity."

"Be that as it may," Tom responded, "like <u>Inherit The Wind</u>, it would be an exciting landmark malpractice case brought against Cro-Academia for bamboozling the Hoi Polloi!"

The Biggest Hissy Fit.

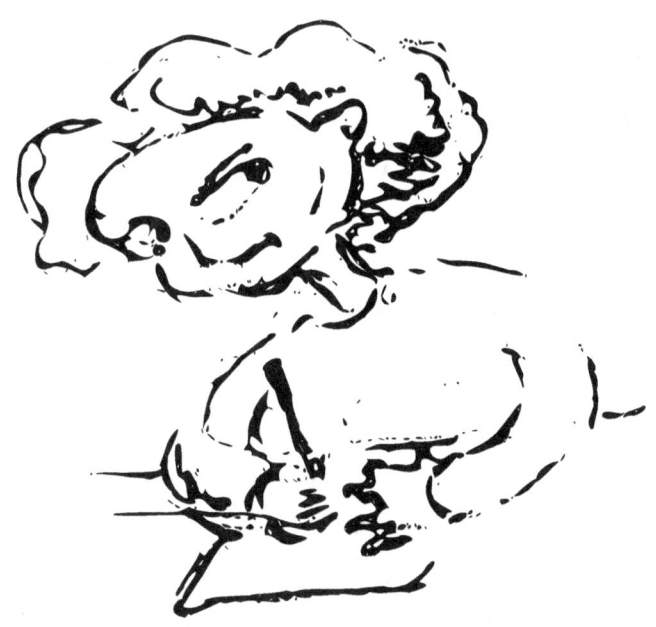

Any illusions Becky and Tom may have held about art and culture prior to their conversation was now water long passed under the hypothetical bridge.

However, Becky and Tom also recognized the conditions for a Renaissance were favorable, while at the same time they understood creative conversations are always overshadowed by distractions clogging the commons, because the arts are not a bombastic process, and thus the subtle evolution of mind goes unnoticed by the Hoi Polloi, until it can't be denied.

The Hoi Polloi can certainly deny the corruption in their academic institutions, but they can not ignore the consequences of their denial, any more than they can deny their inherent nature, because water in the Delta always finds its equilibrium, without regard to being consciously aware.

As I stated initially, I would venture to say, Becky and Tom understand human nature better then anyone I have ever met. And throughout their conversation, as grueling as it was, neither of them ever lost sight of their humanity or sense of humor.

Following this point in Becky's and Tom's conversation, they were focused more on fleshing out the distinction between the metaphorical and hypothetical minds, and less on Becky's issue with the 'others', which was ostensively resolved.

Tom continued speaking about Chauvet's first words in a conversation initiated 40 millenniums past. And believe you me, Becky and Tom were not speaking academically.

"Chauvet was written in the Second-Language," Tom said, "that is syntactically rich, which I mentioned previously, is the core of language. Because, if you do not understand a human's sexual syntax, you will never understand the

Second-Language of Chauvet, or the First-Language of your dreams."

"Syntax," Tom stated, "is the Delta's grammar that threads ideas with life's logic. When we stare in a dream that is a challenge, which is why you told me last week, 'take a picture, it will last longer.'"

"Yea," stated Becky with a look of astonishment, "apparently, you had a storm in your Delta, because you were checking me out!"

"However," Tom said while laughing, "when I glanced at you earlier today, I was simply acknowledging you presence, which did not arouse your ire."

"Looking can also be a question," Tom said. "There are many ways to look and see, like imagining ourself engaged in an activity, which is a point of view that compels our imagination to be both objective and subjective."

"In other words," continued Tom, "like a predator, I patiently observed the subconscious mind's processes by observing how it viewed its ideas, but not to what it was looking at. What one discovers during that deep self reflection, is how the mind operates and makes its case."

"You are making your own case and conversing with yourself," stated Becky.

"True," responded Tom, "but, it's a human way of viewing its world, couched in worldly grammar for untold millenniums, not an upstart's hypothetical blather that always begins with the if-then Wonder-World construct."

"The probative domain of the human mind," Tom said, "is void of behavioral mind conditioning. That's what imagination and dreams are, good old fashion human curiosity that brings the entire Delta to bear on our concern, with a logos as deep as the Wine Dark Sea."

"Imagining ourselves flying treetop level over the Delta," Tom stated, "from that bird-actual overview, which is an amazing mind, because it's a synthesis of the pragmatic and the imaginative domains, when viewing our issue from that purchase, and as we are selecting various striations to explore, those purely pragmatic interactions are relationally imbued with visceral significance from the imaginative heights."

"Then," Tom pointed out, "when familiar circumstance arises in our day-to-day life, our mind will engender an immediate and emotionally apropos mind-set with all of its associated memories for that situation and setting, because of that precognition. That's how the pragmatic aspect of our mind is designed to function; to be metaphorically telluric, imbued with worldly significance, not supersaturated with flicker inducing hypothetical hallucinations."

"I agree," stated Becky, "however, when those emotions are contradictory, that's when my Religion comes alive. It's the sweet-spot when my mind gets, … well, colorful."

"Absolutely," Tom returned coyly, "It's contradictory emotions that stir up a storm in the Delta, like when I was checking you out, because I was swimming in uncharted waters!"

"Yea," stated Becky with one eyebrow raised. "Next you're going to tell me that it was the probative aspect of your mind exploring the possibilities!"

"One dreams," Tom said humorously. "It's the probative aspect of our mind's entire raison dêtre. It's not designed to do the pragmatic day-to-day thing —it's the vanguard."

"When we engage our mind with such challenging questions," continued Tom, "as you say, it gets colorful, which essentially is a conversation with ourselves, a monologue, if you will."

"However," stated Becky, "when we engage in the doing aspect of the creative process, that's a work of art that becomes a dialogue, because we are engaged in a social conversation with the 'others.'"

"Absolutely," Tom said. "The former is the First-Language and the latter is the Second-Language."

"What's the difference between them," asked Becky?

"The only difference between the First and Second-Language," Tom said, "is the distinction between personal and social meaning, where metaphorical expressions are run through a filter of shared experiential meaning. That is to say, not your playful and loving appaloosa, but horseness, which metaphorically means knowledge of movement."

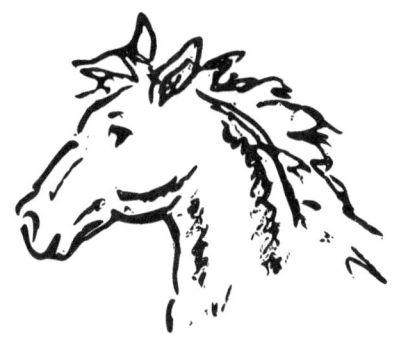

"That makes sense," stated Becky. "Like the way children learn to initially communicate via drawing, the social language would have developed in the same way."

"I would imagine so," Tom said.

"However," Tom stipulated, "that social process took a long time, and contrary to the ridiculous academic assertion that social memories are open to debate, language is not a consensual social process."

"I hope it's clear why that's a non-sequitur," stated Tom. "That is, you can not have a debate about that which makes debating possible. It's sacrosanct, and thus impregnable to assault or trespass. Being trained in a language is contrary to language's primary function of speaking in time."

"There ain't any druthers about that," reiterated Becky, "I learned that the hard way, the day I made the momentous mistake of trespassing on a child deeply engaged in drawing."

"As an artist," Becky admitted, "I should have known not to carelessly recommend to a child their drawing needed a bit more ah-ha, if it was ever going to take off. That momentary lapse in judgment was followed by the biggest hissy fit I have ever experienced."

"Yes, that's a definite no-no," returned Tom. "Similar to the way you communicate in your art, a child does not speak about their drawing, because their drawing is how they are speaking. And when an academic speaks to them about their metaphorical expressions, which is the natural way humans communicate, what they are really saying is, let's have a chat about how to speak."

"Which, stated Tom, "is not a debate at all, it's the system's tactic of introducing the developing creative mind to their own personal hypothetical fish tank."

"That's the first hypothetical mind training that so difficult for an artist to breach," Becky said.

"Nevertheless," Becky continued, "don't we have to have an agreement that three inches is not nine inches, like how Grandma used to tell everyone at family reunions how Grandpa got confused about his ability to measure correctly?"

Tom laughed, and stated, "Now who's the one dragging Grandma and Grandpa, through the mud? Imagining Grandpa reaching for the Viagra® to give Grandma a good shagging is just flat-out disturbing!"

"You're right" returned Becky. "It's my turn to apologize. But, what about the numbers?"

"Well," Tom stipulated, "the natural mind developed mathematical ratios during the Paleolithic age, but they never used math as a language or its syntax, they used it as a Cartesian mind system that aided in their metaphorical linguistic expressions in practical ways, like dates, and quantitative values. However, they were very aware of its paradoxical nature; meaning, if an academic uses math to lend support for some wild hypothetical assertion, I am OK with that. But, if they use their numbers as proof, they are barking up the wrong metaphorical tree!"

"Moreover" Tom said, "as the natural mind certainly understands quantity, like how a child diligently draws numerous pickets to their house's fence, the developing mind is built for more meaningful questions than counting the exact number of pickets."

"What you are talking about," Tom suggested, "is the language and concerns of a Cartesian grocery clerk. Which is to say, math is not perceivable, and thus it can not be language, because it's a product of languaging, which is just another word for imagination. Math, or distinctness, is the Cartesian brother to its non-Cartesian sister of relational recognition of 'sameness,' from which we develop our taxonomy."

"That is to say," stated Tom, "the First and Second-Language's metaphorical words hold embodied significance. Without our mind being firmly rooted in that meaningful ground, it's impossible for it to hypothetically speculate."

"Therefore," Tom emphasized, "the hypothetical cart must always follow the metaphorical horse. Likewise, metaphorical expressions are not open for debate, any more than a child's drawing."

"Try explaining that to the mind that hypothetically hypothesizes," interjected Becky.

"That's what they do," Tom stated, "because they think in systematic terms, which is also why academia's hypothetical Third-Language can certainly be debated. They can Willy Nilly change the meaning of a word like 'female' in their hypothetical construct, and butcher its pronouns till the cows come home, because it's meaningless. It's a hypothetical way of speaking that is untethered from meaningful metaphorical terra firma —for millenniums!"

"To use their reticent parlance," quipped Becky, "it's not a language, it is a language system. Hence, it can be violated ten ways from Sunday, if the system so requires."

Hypothetical Piggies go to Market.

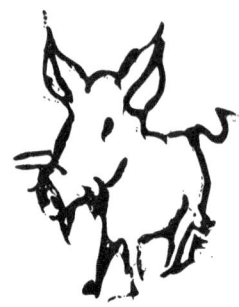

"Subsequently," Tom explained, "if the system deems it useful to alter the spurious hypothetical certainty of the Hoi Polloi, it simply mangles the relevant words in the Third-Language to suit its goals, adding a bit of fear to kick start the process, mixes in an additional smattering of various advertising techniques, like bandwagon, and off the hypothetical piggies go to market!"

"Which is another reason to never take hypothetical hallucinations too seriously," stated Becky. "The combination of their opportunistic logic, in context to their prosaic generative manner of learning is a deteriorating process."

"Let me see if I am catching your drift," continued Becky. "To the hypothetical mind, what is meaningful is not on the bill of fare. Consequently, they want their repast posthaste, and plumb refuse to listen to any meaningful delay."

"Bingo!" Exclaimed Tom. "And by the way, how's your tender follicles?"

"Fine," responded Becky. "Nary one fell out. But, my hair did appreciably curl, as your exposition of the human mind is a bit disturbing. Apparently, the creative mind can be dissuaded from its natural course of action with a blue plate special."

"Nevertheless," Becky continued, "it appears to me, from what you have explained so far, about how the natural mind operates, it's slower than molasses on a cold Winter's day."

"That true," returned Tom. "Building what is meaningful is unquestionably a time consuming process. But what's the rush? Exploring all of the possible scenarios in an embodied way, is a more circumspect crow's-nest from which to plot a course."

"I get it," Becky said, "to the hypothetical mind, it's not about what is meaningful or real, it's exclusively about what is the most expediently profitable, and damn all of the consequences."

"I think so," responded Tom, "academics are not the altruistic sainted deep thinkers they want us to believe they are, or they believe themselves to be."

"Apparently," stated Becky, "today's academics are more akin to corporate shills."

"Then the question becomes," Tom said, "whom among us is so utterly hypothetically beguiled as to listen to a bean counting grocery clerk wax philosophical about the nature of 'all things'?"

To which Becky quipped, "I would say the distracted Hoi Polloi is gullible as all get-out! But let's face it, their porch light may be on, but nobody has been home for millenniums."

"Academics," said Tom, "are acutely aware that the most expedient way to control creative human beings is by bamboozling them. The most opportune time to do that is when their mind is developing, trusting and impressionable –K-3. Meaning, the system is not developing the human mind, it's shaping it as a tool for market!"

"Hence," Tom concluded, "the hypothetically trained mind, being forged into a consummate tool, that's prone to hallucinatory flickering, and stripped of its capacity to build meaningful metaphorical knowledge, is now susceptible to any utilitarian assertion, such as art was born from some primal bodily function that needs to be expressed!"

"Jesus wept," exclaimed Becky, "that's up there with convincing a bird that flying is hazardous to its health!"

"Nevertheless," Tom stated, "that's the verity of the matter! Art, or to be more pedantic, the technological display of salient social memories, was born under exigent circumstances, because it was about surviving during a glacial period. Thus, I see art for what it actually was, it was mind-tech that extended the mortal reach of the human mind socially, which helped them survive an unforgiving world."

"Unbelievable," exclaimed Becky. "Like the netting of a gathering of fish, academia's pond rippling think tanks are euphemistically promulgated as schools!"

"It's a hilarious state of affairs," returned Tom. That a creative being has swallowed the personified hook, the entire hypothetical line of BS, and the symbolic sinker!"

A PRICKLY POSTURE!

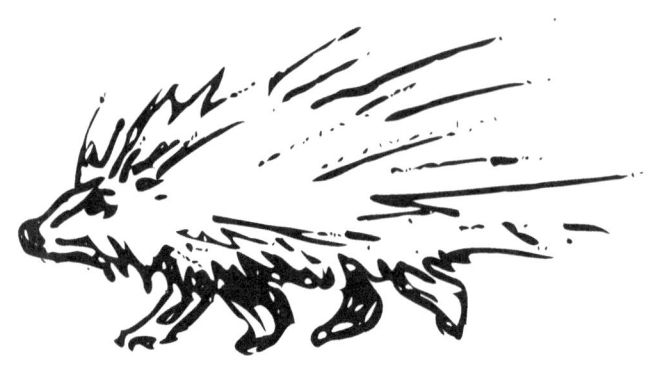

"I'm not even going to tell you how I feel about a creative human being gallivanting through life as a Tuffy Tool® in some academic's toolbox," stated Becky. "But, I'll tell you what, ever since water-walkers 'privatized' our language, we have been barkin' up the wrong tree. It's not, if the creek don't rise, but if it's ever going to recede. It never ends with flickers, if it's not the bed bugs, its the ants."

"I see the situation in the same way," Tom said. "The flicker is so mercilessly distracted it wanders aimlessly without instant access to their enthralling beguilement. As where the creative human mind is like a cat, whose passion for life will not stray for any reason from its endeavor."

"Which is ironic," Tom pointed out, "as it was our creative capacity that built civilization, which was subsequently transfigured by water-walkers into a hive-minded gizmo, eviscerating its creative capacity, and as you say, like a crab, it now walks backward waging war with everyone and everything including itself."

"It walks backwards alright," stated Becky, "albeit quicker than a roach when the light comes on!"

"And that's the real danger," added Tom, "considering our technology moves things along so quickly. That speed, combined with careless decisions due to a missing compiler is a recipe for an accident waiting to happen."

Becky interjected, "We need to stop pussy-footing around with these myopically distracted fools, like how Grandma laid down the law to Grandpa. She would never allow him to drive the car with his Coke bottle like spectacles; who didn't have a lick of sense as to which way to turn."

"Obviously," continued Becky, "that never stopped Grandpa from hollerin' at Grandma at every opportunity, telling her to turn straight into this or that ditch."

"Well," said Tom, "they have been driving us into one ditch after another for millenniums. You would think they might have enough sense to let us drive for a bit."

"Yea, when the cows come home," returned Becky. "Grandma had to actually drag Grandpa out from behind the wheel, kickin' an' screamin', each and every time we was fixin' to go hither or yon."

The Sovereign and the Bean Counter.

"I'm up a stump as to how to contend with the insanity," stated Becky. "We are living in a cultural desert that's so dried-up, the trees are bribing the dogs!"

"Well," Tom said, as he smiled, "we are up against thousand of years of hive-mind classical Pavlovian behavioral conditioning, with peer reviewing, virtual signaling support groups, merciless distractions and academia's eternal assaults on the metaphorical mind."

"The other day," Becky stated with an expression of disbelief, "I asked an octogenarian what was life like before TV, and his answer was, 'it was boring,' if you can believe that!"

"Now I ask you," Becky said, "as an artist, whose passion for life is the source of my Religion, how can I possibility have a conversation with a distracted gizmo that considers life boring?"

"Back in the day," Becky said, "when I was a little girl traveling to school, I walked alone for about a quarter a mile along a gravel road with no lights or homes to get to the paved road to catch the school bus. During that walk each morning I stepped briskly as not to show fear to the immense forest that dominated both sides of the way.

"On one dark burrvous winter's morning, so cold the snow squeaked under foot," Becky said in a softening tone, "while waiting for the bus to arrive," Becky exclaimed loudly, "a stag the size of a horse with a full rack of antlers burst into the clearing, so close I could hear his thunderous breath as he issued clouds of steam from his flaring nostrils. He briefly acknowledge my presence while catching his breath then continued on his way as the steam from his breath swirled in his wake."

"That lived experience," stated Becky, "made me feel so alive that I still dream of that moment as a metaphorical expression of the significance of moments in time, which was anything but boring, like the nonsense they taught us in school."

"It's frustrating," Tom said, "but we can't force them to listen any more than we can pry them away from their Cell or TV. They are addicted to being constantly stimulated with ever increasing intensity to maintain the efficacy of their derangement!"

"The only possibility of reaching the human mind," stated Tom, "is if they hold a spark of interest in life, like children. But, as we have established, academia does a bang up job of exsanguinating them of their life force, as academia has been processing human minds into hybrids for millenniums."

"Ergo," stated Becky sadly, "the only thing an artist can do is inspire."

"Only," Tom exclaimed, "it's not just the only thing you can do, it's the one and only thing you ever need to do. Hypothetically speaking, you are holding the staff of God woman that can part the Wine Dark Sea!"

"With all of their mind training, tricks and millenniums of intrigues," Tom said, "the only thing they can do is distract, mislead and incite discord. It's from your creative ability to inspire the human mind is what civilization is built on and that is why they attack the Delta with such a vengeance; water-walkers were never in control nor will they ever be. The only reason they endure like roaches is they entrench themselves in vital social systems."

"You are right," Becky said, "They succeeded in overwhelming me and I lost sight of the importance of what I do —Thanks."

"Any time," said Tom. "Add that to your ten commandments."

"Right," Becky responded. "Thou shalt not lose sight of one's lodestar."

"Accordingly," Tom stated, "if only as a form of self preservation, to ensure we are thinking clearly, we need to talk more about the formidable natural design of the First-Language, which the Second-Language maintains its connection via the metaphorical."

"I'm glad you are going to expound on that, because it was not entirely clear to me when you spoke about the various languages," interjected Becky.

"Sure," responded Tom, "Like most mammals, the First-Language refers to the natural biological process of our mind; no training is required —just life."

"Like the First-Language," Tom stipulated, "the Second-Language, that is art, does not require training, because like life, the Second-Language is its reflection. It's experiential."

"However," Tom pointed out, "the Third-Language, being a hypothetically personified hive-mind system, has lost its connection to the land of the living."

"While the Fourth-Language," Tom said, "that is —AI, is simply the Third-Language's automation, because the hypothetical mind, as wound up as it is, even they can't keep up with the complexity of their leviathan."

"Obviously," continued Becky, "using robotics and AI to automate the entire process is more expedient, and thus it's the most profitable way to proceed in reaping future harvests, and as schooling every generation is a very big expense, we understand the system's intentions."

"You aptly defined today's social circus," returned Tom. "We have a culture teaming with obsolete Third-Language trained Tuffy Tools®, and as the system's only governor is the bottom line, making plans for those tools was never on its itinerary. Likewise, the system does not know what to do with them, any more than they know what to do with themselves."

"Predictably," Tom stated, "the system gamed out, the most expedient and efficient way to deal with them is to distract the bejesus out of them!"

"Those Tuffy Tools®, stated Becky, "will either have to rediscover their creative capacity to build their own meaningful future, or be subjugated by the system's escalating distractions, which invariably ends in a big bada boom!"

"However," stated Tom, "there is a significant caveat before one can embark on the greatest adventure of their lives. It requires a compiler, that's not on the market for sale at any price."

"The Second-Language," Tom stated, "requires a DIY (do it yourself) self awareness reeducation in the human mind to understand how to use it with any degree of sincerity."

"As I previously suggested," said Tom, "the Second-Language maintains its connection via the metaphorical to the First-Language's logic, which threads its concerns into three distinct minds; the imaginative mind, the behavioral oriented like pragmatic mind, along with a limbic mind, that's like a governor, if you will."

"The governor," stated Tom, "bridges the various accepts of our mind, which is not limited to visual intelligence, i.e., imagination; making the limbic system, or governor, the core of our creative intellect."

"In other words," Tom said, "our imagination sees in an emotionally fragrant way, because our aural and olfactory intellects are imbued into our visual intelligence via emotions and memories."

"Obviously," Tom said, "our aural sensibility engenders emotional meaning. But, it's our olfactory sensibility that is by far the most interesting."

"What the proboscis does," Tom said, "can not be defined. It is the 'like sense' that is to say, it's the associated aspect of our intellect."

"You're right," Becky responded. "It is impossible to define or describe an odor. We have to associate it with something else. However, I never thought of the olfactory it those terms. That is, our sensibility that facilitates relational meaning."

"Try it sometime," stated Tom. "Change your venue and smell the various fragrances you encounter deeply, which will immediately fire-up the visual boiler of your imagination. That's why Gramps can't remember a damn thing, he lost his sense of smell and his mind along with it!"

"It's the olfactory that imbues relational meaning into our imaginative apperception," stated Tom, "like seeing a horse in the clouds, which is one of the many limbic states of mind, that's like being aware of your awareness."

"If you want to understand your mind's syntax, pay close attention to what the governor does, and when it does it," explained Tom, "which always comes alive when we use all of our senses probatively, void of distractions, and the best way to define that process is, by being aware of your apperception."

"Jesus wept," exclaimed Becky. "That's another triple mental somersault, instead of being hypothetical it's now metaphorical!"

"I know," returned Tom, "it sounds impossible, but, it's actually quite doable. Because we are not fighting the Delta's current, we are going with its flow. Most importantly, our mind is designed to function in that manner."

"Necessarily," Tom pointed out, "it doesn't occur all at once. It's more of a continual process improvement that has to be built, because we are born with a capacity, not an ability. Just because you own a bicycle doesn't mean you know how to ride."

"Moreover," stated Tom, "the governor will recognize what you are doing and will assist you. To use your parlance Becky, 'it's plumb slapped out of spending a lifetime conversing with a hypothetical bonehead!'"

"The governor," continued Tom, "emotionally threads concepts, and previous experiential memories, to imbue greater contextual meaning to the present context. Seeing a horse in a cloud, is the imaginative aspect of our mind and governor stating the environment is changing."

"To be honest," interjected Becky, "I never fully recognized the amazing capacity of our natural mind. Academics always told me the horse in the cloud was a vestige of a primitive mind."

"That's rich," returned Tom. "That a hypothetical upstart would bandy about the word primitive when addressing its sovereign, when it feels threatened by it, can't stop rebelling against it, and is eternally laying siege to it. I have to ask the obvious question, what in hell is academia's definition of primitive?"

"Well," answered Becky, "I would have ...

"I was being rhetorical," interrupted Tom!

"Yea, I got that," stated Becky. "But, what I was going to say is, academia has no imagination and thus it can never build an identity, much less an original idea. Hence, academia's character is that of a petulantly capricious child, perpetually engaged in Delta mud slinging."

"Yet," Tom said, "with all of their destructive intrigues, our biological mind still speaks to us with an alacrity. It was the imaginative mind that determined the environment was changing, not the personified, catch-as-catch-can hypothesis of the incomplete action thinking of a bean counter."

"The bean counter," continued Tom, "agonizing over their obliviousness, proceeds to blame-shift their shortcomings on, … wait for it … that's right, … you guessed it, their sovereign, which has survived countless glaciations, long before the hybrid was an irritating speck in the creative mind's eye."

"It's the natural human mind," Tom said, "that always makes meaningful determinations. And if we do not aqueous to its recommendations, or listen with a degree of sincerity to the upstart's hypothetical prattle, or its mechanical shadow (AI), it will treat us to a nightmare."

"If the natural mind determines the hypothetical mind has become so rudderless, that the situation has become exigent," Tom stipulated, "it will wine and dine us into a nervous break-down, which will send us screaming into the hills, or to our local therapist, who will subsequently send us to the pharmacist to sedate our sovereign!"

"If everyone understood that," added Becky, "like my Grandma, every grocery clerk would be dragged out from behind the wheel of the cultural bus, kicking and screaming."

"It's unfortunate the academic mind is so immature," stated Becky. "Like the limbic system, we could build a bridge linking the two minds."

"As interesting as your thinking is," said Tom, "I do not think that is the answer. They are a twisted product of the creative mind that has undergone two evolutions away from its metaphorical root, and in the process of undergoing its final evolution to, … well to put it bluntly, irrelevancy. We speak diametrically opposed languages. The only amenable resolution would be similar to the sun and the moon that share the same sky but never together and definitely not in the same orbit."

"Your right of course," Becky said. "We don't beguile the Hoi Polloi, tell them how to think, or what to do; we inspire them to think and do for themselves."

"However," Tom stipulated, "in order to do what we do, we need to clearly understand how the creative human mind functions as well as having an unobstructed view of the opposition's efforts to undermine our endeavors."

"Excluding the limbic system, aka the governor," Tom stated, "our natural mind has basically two distinct functional modes. The first is the imaginative and the second is the behavioral."

"That is to say, a thinking about thinking mind," Tom said, "called imagination, and a doing-thinking mind that has no probative value, and thus it relies on emotions, instinct, and learned behavior, which are built from, … that's right, … the governor."

"Predictably," stated Becky, "academia has no choice but to train the behavioral aspect of our mind with no probative value whatsoever. Because, like a lioness, the imaginative aspect of our mind can not be trained to perform in academia's social circus. Which means academic duplicity is crafted to usurp the Delta to supplant it as mentor to the Cartesian mind."

"Right," Tom returned, "the mind that imagined the horse in the clouds, involved the governor linking it with its behavior like pragmatic counterpart to get busy, i.e., get out of the way of the approaching storm. And please, try not to drive straight into a hypothetical ditch while you do it, which was metaphorically suggested by the horse in the cloud morphing into a loving mother and child!"

"What I'm saying," continued Tom, "is knowledge is not a hypothetical thing, it's part of our being, as much as the water we drink and the air we breath. Concepts like the eternal, was not gifted to us by some hypothetically flickering loon, it is inherently understood by the natural mind, which was metaphorically expressed in the cave of Chauvet during the Paleolithic period."

"As such," Tom stated, "all beings are knowledge, like the fish is the water being. If you want to know about water, that is your mind, don't talk to an idiot like Thales, talk to a fish, because its entire evolutionary trajectory is immersed in water."

"Speaking of watery evolutionary trajectories," interrupted Becky, "my eyeballs are floatin', I have a powerful need to visit the sandbox. After which, I'm fixin' to refresh my drink. How yours?"

"Empty," Tom answered, and began to laugh, because he realized from Becky's comment he may have gone a bit overboard in contextualizing Becky's 'issue' with the 'others'. After a brief break and another refreshment, Tom began to wrap it up

. . .

Their Proboscis Worked Just Fine!

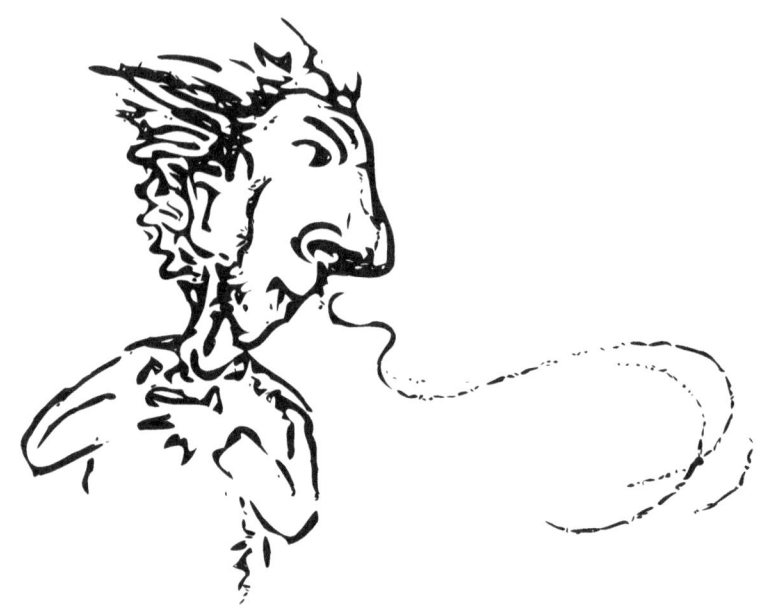

"The limbic mind or governor," Tom summarized, "is the kernel of our creative mind. It's the wellspring from which the sum total of our lived experiences supports us in how we are presently being imaginatively or pragmatically mindful. Are we hearing, or are we listening intently, with great expectations?"

"The pragmatic mind," Tom explained, "be it actual or imaginatively experiential, which can be an amazing mind, as it is the proving ground for the imaginatively speculative mind's ideas, if our imagined actions come into direct conflict with the limbic governor's many states of mind, with its array of voices, all hell can break loose."

"That's when the hunter becomes the hunted in our imaginative dreams," Tom stated. "Meaning, that nightmare you franticly experienced was a consequence of you having a really silly idea, in which that three pronged mental validation process was splainin' it to ya!"

"I had a few of those dreams myself," claimed Becky. "So what you are saying is, my mind was telling me, 'you may want to put that bright hypothetical idea on the back burner — permanently!'"

"I think so," returned Tom. "The creative mind is sovereign, and it will not be hypothetically shushed, by any pond rippler, including its hypothetically trained counterpart."

"Furthermore," Tom suggested, "when we recognize the Third-Language's validation process is non-existent, as it has a singular hypothetical mind, with incomplete thinking, littered with fallacies, groceries lists, drifting logic, hypothetical nouns, all of which are uprooted from reality and what is meaningful, which is what makes life worth living, and considering they are expediting the insanity by rushing to the Fourth-Language(AI), with an army of obsolete Tuffy Tool® minded types being mercilessly distracted, we understand the exigent nature of the social problem."

"Like Icarus," Tom elaborated, "apparently none of its meaningless ideas get put on the back burner. The only governor the hypothetical mind recognizes or values is, can it be shipped to market in the most expedient fashion!"

Becky interjected, "Are you saying, that without meaningful intervention, our natural way of thinking will be shunned like a bastard at a family reunion? Which to me sounds no different than the present situation."

"Yes, that's true," acknowledged Tom, "but, with the transformation to the Fourth-Language(AI), that situation will deteriorate exponentially, because interacting with an AI machine programed with a dead Third-Language, is a foregone conclusion. Yet, as frustrating as it is conversing with a hypothetical bonehead, hybrids do maintain a gossamer thread to their humanity."

"What I'm saying," stated Tom, "if you think selfie wielding, texting over sharing fingers, Jonesing to know the latest distraction, GPS tracked, virtually signaling beguiled system plugged snitches, void of interlocutor in brain, whom are reality adverse with a metaphorically challenged symbolic hive-mind in their back pocket hoards are frighting, you ain't seen nothin' yet!"

"What will soon follow," Tom warned, "will be a meaningless technological social nightmare, which will cause social disintegration, and subsequently war! But then again, it's beginning to look more like a pharmacological get your latest injection update dystopia in a Brave New World of sedated sovereigns, or worse, genetically eviscerated sovereigns —GMM!"

"Don't you mean GMO's," asked Becky?

"No," responded Tom, "a GMM, a Genetically Modified Mind. As their training makes them oblivious to their metaphorical faculties, they would also be oblivious to the evisceration of that aspect of their being and thus, for all intents and purposes, their decedents will be cattle."

"Well," returned Becky, "under those circumstances, a Tuffy Tool® will likely be as happy as a dead pig in the sunshine, but as a creative type, that makes my blood boil; as that's about as gruesome of an assault on our creative nature as one could possibility imagine, which also means academia is no longer just a millstone around our neck, they are now an existential threat."

"However, continued Becky, "and on a brighter note, I was pleasantly surprised with the level of resistance by so many independent minds that risked it all, when they outright refused to comply with the system's 'vial' covid crusade."

"Those brave souls," continued Becky, "bless their hearts, may have been missing their compiler, but their proboscis worked just fine."

"The question now," Becky concluded, "is how do we wish to proceed? Are we to continue imbibing on hypothetical moonshine, or would we prefer to sip on a fine sparkling wine, while we metaphorically dine?"

"Speaking of dining, I'm plumb slapped out and hungry as a horse," stated Becky, "meaning, I need to feed at the trough!"

"Me too," returned Tom. "We can pick up this conversation another time. But I am wondering, did we resolve anything?"

"Not a cotton pickin' thing," stated Becky. "But, we did conclusively identify the problem, and raised some interesting possibilities, and that's as fine as a frog's hair split two ways!"

"See ya' Becky, and don't forget my big box of crayons!"

"I fixin' to get right on that … Later Tom."

WHAT'S PAST IS PROLOGUE:

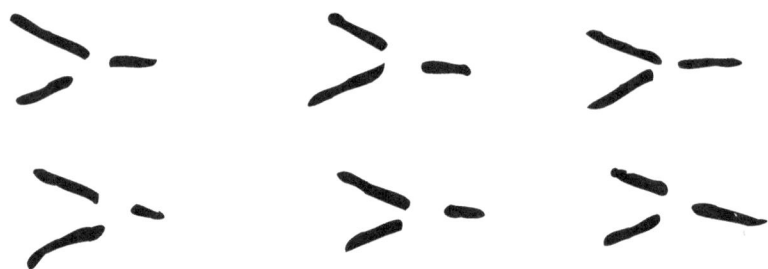

Becky's and Tom's conversation about 'all things', I found inspirational, but disturbing. Obviously, how we are mindful about 'all things' determines our destiny. Without a compiler, our future will certainly be profitable, but feeding is not living; it's entirely enduring, which is a tawdry legacy, for a purportedly creative being that lost its proverbial mind to tech.

As Becky would say, "don't get me wrong," tech is great; yet, a being that permits itself to be ruled by it, or allows itself to be perpetually distracted, and thus lives in constant turmoil, can never be the architect and master of their own mind, or forge a meaningful destiny. Dining on the other hand, if only on a slice of stale metaphorical bread, is to begin to show signs of life; dare I say 'woke' from its eternal hypothetical slumber.

My recommendation to academia, besides running their cell-phones and minds through the rinse cycle, is a remedial reading of, <u>Dream Duet</u>. That is, if academia wishes to maintain a modicum of credibility for when their social storm resolves, and it will.

Otherwise, it will become another meaningless institutional fossil like the Church, which was the academic institution during the time of the Gutenberg Press.

The academic institution during the age of the Internet, is the Corporation, as they set all systematic curriculum. Likewise, it too falsely assumes it holds a monopoly on something called the truth, they call it 'prophets', which may be more refreshing than their holier than thou predecessor's, because they flat out state the obvious, bold as brass —they worship the banquet!

However, what remained the same was how both institutions infantilized human culture, because both lost control of the Third-Language to the mind-tech of their era.

Jo-Jo would claim, "It's the hypothetical Thing Man, you know the Thing's Thingness MAN, COME ON!"

Becky would respond to such high minded buffoonery by stating, "Jo-Jo, being the system's Huckleberry, was simply having a dying duck fit, gaffing his way to perdition, while inviting apparatchiks to fly their ducks to a bad pond of water."

As far as Becky reckoned, "Their just blowin' up another systematic storm that has been brewing through the ages. Most believe they are fighting in the latest valiant battle against this or that Sam Hill grocery clerk, that fell out of the hypothetical ugly tree, and hit every damn branch on the way down. But the plumb fact of the matter is, they are embroiled with another species core-tech, and thus they got a permanent hitch in their get-along."

"The verity of the matter," Tom would say, "is human identity does not manifest Willy Nilly from some ability or characteristic we were born with. We must courageously stand on our own two feet to consciously build and shape our identity from our creative capacity, which demands a deep metaphorical dive into one's inherent nature."

Mr. Samuel Langhorne Clemens would agree with Becky and Tom and would likely suggest, "History doesn't repeat itself, but it sho-nuff does rhyme!

And whatever y'all do, please, for the love of what makes life worth living, tell the Sam Hill grocery clerks, they're 'bout half a bubble off plumb!"

As narrator of this bodacious event, I will say, you just read the latest in a long line of artistic polemics assaulting the high walls of academia and its religious hive-minded hypocrisy, which dates back to the time when Geoffrey Chaucer laid siege to the academy of his day —the Church.

And yes, I too have high hopes that a meaningful Renaissance will soon follow the current academic Dark Age, where our real identity as creative beings will be explored and celebrated, not repressed with eternal assaults on our creative nature, or hypothetical virtual identity politics of race and sexuality crafted to infantilize human culture.

Becky calls it her Religion, Tom calls it his Mojo, Mr. Clemens called it his Mark-Twain! However, they all agreed the recipe for living life to its fullest, without regrets, was to follow their bow legged Grandmas' loving advise, "can't never could."

I will end the conversation with a treasured performance by Shemp and company in the <u>Knights of the Round Table</u>, which to me embodies the solution to all of our problems, past, present, and future, "An-a-one, an-a-two, an-a-sooow … weeee … stuck our little tootsies in the wa-ter, and we dunked under the waves we did – Ha –Ha!"

Cheers! E.D.

ARTIST AUTHOR.

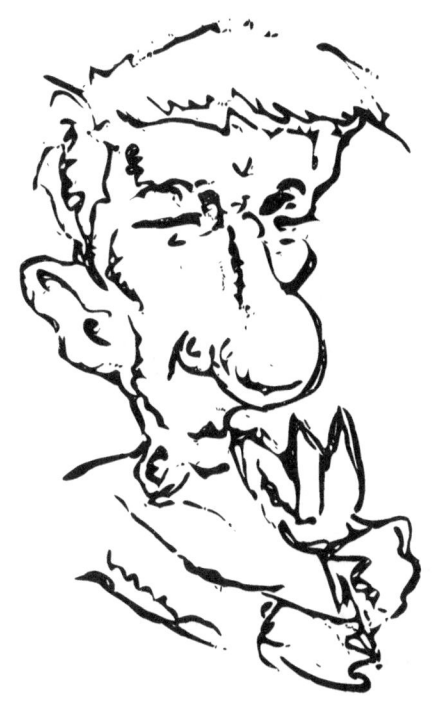

—Edmund Dalpe, MFA., artist-author of <u>Dream Duet</u>, 2017, which is a guide in building mind bridges; bridging the modern trained mind with the ancient metaphorical, the conscious with the subconscious, the theoretical with the experiential, the individual with the social. In short, Dream Duet is about cultivating your Religion, Mojo, or Mark-Twain!

The following is a small excerpt from <u>Dream Duet</u> to give you an idea of what to expect:

The Long Reflection of the Lioness ...

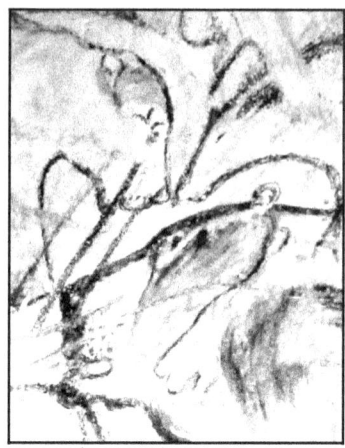

Chauvet. (Valette, 2017) (CC)

The cave of Chauvet was/is pure dream speak. One in which the central character, the Lioness, would build the foundation of a greater human awareness. And like all good stories, the story of Chauvet begins at its end, when the Lioness had walked for so long and so far, she was confronted with her own mortality, when her once powerful actions slowed to a crawl, like the Great Rhinoceros, and her sharp vision of youth was now fading with age.

When the Lioness recognized she would be incapable of finishing the great task she envisioned for herself, of witnessing and thus understanding the galactic cycle in fullness, she became deeply saddened that such a journey was beyond the capability of a mortal. She became restless. Her dreams filled with images of water, of turquoise waves that swelled as high as mountains, where she encountered winged lions of stone, that spoke in unintelligible tongues beneath the deep.

The Lioness was overwhelmed by the dreams that flooded her mind. Until one day, while drinking from a pool of water, they made perfect sense. She understood their meaning; that she could speak about her great vision on the cave walls, so that her children's children's children could see her life's journey, the way she saw her own reflections in the pool of water. Likewise, they would know her mind and the bold vision she began so long ago would never die.

Long after the great Lioness was a distant memory, and her children's children's children were forgotten in time, a child was born with the same bold curiosity about the galaxy, that the Great Lioness possessed. However, unlike the Lioness' reflections from so long ago, the galaxy during the time of the yearling was very different. It was beginning to rear up, as if poised to do something.

From the Lioness' reflections, the yearling realized the galaxy changes imperceptibly over a lifetime, but its movement could be recognized over many lifetimes. She then understood the greatness of the Lioness' vision, that the Lioness wasn't speaking about the nature of the galaxy, per se, she was speaking about speaking itself, long speaking, speaking across oceans of time.

And like the Great Lioness, she kept a watchful eye on the galaxy and recorded her vision alongside of her ancestor's, all of the years of her life. And so the torch was past down through the ages, from one generation to the next, like the rings of a great tree, which continued to expand and grow outward.

Many generations hence, so many that the Stag of Ages grew two enormously long silvery beards, and the great cave of reflections was filled with visions of the countless generations, they had arrived at the same place, but in a very different time that the Great Lioness began so long ago, and understood the fullness of her journey for the very first time.

As previously stated, in context to the other two great caves of the Stone-Age, Altamira and Lascaux, Chauvet was preschool. Yet, the truth is, Chauvet is the most amazing of all of the caves, because it's the genesis of self awareness and its application in building knowledge of the ages, that is, Chauvet is the Lion's Gait; the lion's stride!